KNOW THE

ONLY TRUTH

DISRUPTIVE CONSCIOUSNESS

INTRODUCTION

Some things will always end up escaping our traditional understanding because we are so conditioned. And we have been so for many generations. It may be that now with the massive access to a lot of information we begin to know more of what has been hidden, but under this same massiveness is that it becomes difficult to join the dots that lead to discovering certain truths that were hidden.

The one truth, which is why you entered this book, is that there are many truths. Yours, mine, and, what I consider the most powerful of them all, the truth/reality that we all together create as a planetary community.

As much as I dedicate myself to writing about personal development, now and then books like this come to me as a message. I can be brushing my teeth, training, or even just lost in the middle of nowhere or surrounded by lots of people when a thought/idea pops up and whispers to me "this is the title of the new book, write down the table of contents now".

I am passionate about mysteries, I admit it, if it is not that I read or look at something somewhere, I end up reflecting and going to levels where I put my mind in check to realize how limited it ends up being to the physical and three-dimensional.

But without being discouraged, in this book we will talk in-depth about the control that is exercised over all of us at an unconscious level and how this leads these people to be able to "predict" what will happen, or even, we to create those same things that we then catalog as predictions. As a result of this, we will introduce COVID and the pandemic, but more than anything to open our eyes to discover its secret formula of manipulation and not let it rule us anymore. The last two chapters are where we will push our minds to their limit to try to expand the understanding and perspectives, we have of ourselves, the past, the Earth, and the future from there. In these chapters, you can prepare to shatter boundaries and beliefs that were dwelling in your mind were false.

It should be noted that I do not come here as the savior or a God with all the answers you need, nor am I the one who knows the most or knows best.

I just feel that I have a great tool (writing) and a great power of communication with which I can get messages like these to millions of people.

What is my purpose? To uncover my blindfolds more and more to easily connect with my essence and realize that I am a spiritual being living a human experience. That I am not a physical body, but that I am inhabiting one. That I am nothing and no one, but that I am also everything and everyone. And by direct consequence, so are you.

THE HIDDEN ROOT

Aliens created us: real evidence never seen before

Although we will touch on this subject again later, here we will dive right into the evidence of the gigantic possibility that this is true.

At a point in life where there are still billions of people who believe that we were created in a single instant by a single creator, questioning such beliefs will always generate a lot of controversies. As well questioning the scientific community that we are the result of evolution, but regardless of whether they are true or not, here we will see that both have some truth to them.

Many researchers and scientists are beginning to shed light on the issue that we were created by an alien race and that they played a very important role in the evolution of the human race.

Let's take a look at some of the most debated but most incredible discoveries to date:

The Big Bang of the Brain:

In 2004, researchers at the University of Chicago presented the results of a long-term study that concluded that the sophistication of the human brain could not be the result of slow evolution, but had to be the result of rapid dramatic change. They said that some kind of special event occurred 50,000 years ago, and that explains how human culture went from primitive cave drawings to sophisticated civilizations. It is believed that at that time the human brain was separated into two hemispheres and that we acquired the ability to think abstractly. One of the many elements that changed was a unique gene called foxp2, which is responsible for language and our ability to speak. At the time, all animals had it, but it was altered so that humans were able to communicate and think abstractly. If we put it all in perspective, all this also happened at the same time as the cave carvings, our only historical record, show interesting creator gods. Non-human beings that look like aliens. Even more amazing, this happened when Neanderthal man mysteriously became extinct 40,000 years ago.

Our genetic DNA has to be more than luck or chance: biological SETI

Some things were created in such a perfect way that there had to be some artist involved, this seems to be the story of our DNA. In 2013, physicists from Kazakhstan National University said that in human DNA there is a mathematical code so sophisticated that it cannot be explained by evolution, even, though it makes more sense that it was designed by another intelligent life form. Other research published in a prestigious science journal pointed out that human DNA is ordered with mathematical precision and has perfectly ordered patterns of hydrography, which means that our DNA uses symbols to express physical concepts similar to how we use them to convey language, and language is a human construct. The Kazakhstan physicists also suggested something quite radical: the coding of our DNA has remained relatively unchained since our creation. It functions as a filing cabinet to preserve the human design. The physicists think that the coding ports are a kind of receiver like an extraterrestrial satellite dish, which

Biological SETI literally suggests that our bodies are receivers for the presence of extraterrestrial life.

If true, it would be similar to when SETI, in 1977, received a mysterious signal from space, a signal of WOW!

This theory suggests that our bodies are waiting for a signal from these strange creatures, and that when we receive it our biology will know.

Our shared ancestry: "Eve" and beyond:

In the Hebrew Bible, the book of Genesis says that Eve was created from Adam's rib, and was given the breath of life. In more recent years, with more accurate technology to measure our genes, genetic studies have shown amazing things. This has given us a profound insight into our ancestors. There is evidence that every human alive today can trace our lineage back to a common female ancestor of African origin who lived some 200 million years ago. Because studies measure mitochondrial DNA variations against the average mutation rate over time, this common female ancestor is called the Mitochondrial Eve. All of humanity, then, has evolved from one of the two branches that came from Eve. One branch is completely African, and the other contains all other races with some African lineage. Although there are no physical remains of this "Eve", its existence has been confirmed. At one time, one female harbored all of the current extant genes. Mitochondrial Eve was not the first or only female on Earth when she lived. It is believed that a cataclysmic event occurred when she was alive, massively reducing the human population and creating a genetic bottleneck.

What is still not explained is why humans evolved in two completely different ways. What is also elusive is how, after thousands of years, suddenly so many races evolved in such a short period.

RH-negative blood:

In our school years, we have all been taught the basics about blood types and how they work, but they overlook how strange it is when an RH-negative mother goes on to have a baby with RH-positive blood.

If a woman with RH-negative blood becomes pregnant with a baby with RH-positive blood, her body will produce antigens signaling to her immune system that her fetus is toxic. The woman's body will then proceed to kill her child. What is normal about that? Even in nature itself, there is no indication of this kind of biological self-destruction. The natural result of many hybrid animals such as mules and tigers is infertility. Some say that the RH-

negative blood is nothing more than a mutation, but others speculate that it may come from an alien species that interbred with humans or otherwise genetically modified to produce a hybrid bloodline. About 15% of the world's population has Rh-negative blood, but the curious thing is that this percentage of the population is not spread evenly across all areas of the planet. The largest amount, 44% of Rh- negative blood, is located in the Basque region between France and Spain. The Basques are the only people in Western Europe who still speak an Indo- European language, an isolated language that is not spoken anywhere else in Europe. And not only is it isolated, but it is completely unrelated to any other European language.

Another known anomaly is that people with negative HR are more prone to experience psychic phenomena and alien abduction. Also, physically, some characteristics of HR negative, are that they are people with high IQs, heightened intuition, lower body temperature, higher blood pressure, red or reddish hair, sensitivity to sunlight, and sometimes an extra vertebra in their spine.

Since this issue is not talked about and passed off as normal, this distinction is irrelevant today. Still, there is no rational explanation as to why with our overwhelming instinct to procreate, a pregnant woman's body would destroy her creation, unless perhaps nature was part of some manipulation in the past.

"The Missing Link:
As we already know, the most accurate theory today regarding the evolution of man is the one put forward by Darwin, which states that we evolved from apes over thousands of years and that our intellectual abilities were brought into existence by natural selection. He believed that when our ancestors began to walk on two feet, they began to use their hands to make tools. But if evolution occurs slowly over a long period there should be slight changes in our ancestors. But the evidence indicates just the opposite. Almost 6 million years ago, one of the many species of apes stood upright and began to walk on two feet, but then there was no change for 4 million years, until, according to fossil records, the species began to make stone tools, and then there was no advance until almost two million years ago. Until, about 200,000 years ago, homo sapiens, better known as "us", appeared. And there was no small change, but a huge one. If we look at evolutionary histories, they are confusing. They show the evolution of man without showing what has been discovered. If you look at the fossil comparisons, it is clear that there are no transitional species from ape-like creatures that have existed for millions of years to present-day humans.

We should be more likely to find more recent fossils than ancient ones like the famous "Lucy", which dates back more than 3 million years. Where are the more recent transitional beings? Where is this "missing link"?

Considering that alligators have not changed one bit in at least 65 million years, it is possible that the "missing link" is missing because it does not exist. Since a genetic modification made by a more advanced life form is responsible for the leap in our intelligence. This theory could also explain why there are so many different races or versions of humans in just a few thousand years...

Evidence of Direct Panspermia:

In 2011, genetically modified DNA was sent into space from Sweden on the outside of a rocket. When it returned, it had a small microscopic sphere made of Titanium and Vanadium, with a width of human hair that came from space. This article had strands of life on the outside and a sticky substance that contained some kind of biological life coming out of its center. And when the rocket returned to Earth, this particle still contained that life even after being at a temperature of 1000 degrees Celsius. A team of researchers at the University of Buckingham speculated that the biological material contained genetic material, but had no idea where it came from. One theory state that it would be something from what is called Direct Panspermia, which is the spread of living systems through space travel to suitable environments or planets with intelligent life forms in space. This apparent piece of science fiction would probably never have been taken seriously were it not for the fact that it was suggested by scientist Francis Crick, the Nobel Prize nominee for DNA research.

Other researchers were concerned that it might have been intended for a much more sinister purpose: to deliberately spread a life-threatening virus and then send it to Earth with malice. In the end, given its nature and properties, it has all the patterns that indicate it could have been sent intentionally.The Double Helix in Ancient Caverns:

On virtually every continent, wherever there are carvings encrypted among ancient ruins, there are countless numbers of strange giant human hybrids and other creatures portrayed as heavens or gods ofthe hollow Earth, and as the creators of man. Even ifthese images of creator gods were just folklore, howwould you explain the images of a double helix that are also in these ancient carvings?

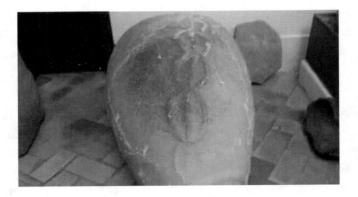

For example, one of the earliest images of a double helix was found carved on a huge round stone of almost two meters, which dates back to 7 thousand years ago. If the image of a double helix was just a coincidence, the fact that the huge stone was molded in the shape of an egg, the symbol of fertility and reproduction, makes it more so. Images of the double helix are also found in Sumerian pictograms from four thousand four hundred years before Christ. Considering the fact that the double helix was not discovered until 1960, it is obvious that someone or something understood precisely what its role was in our body. The double helix symbol, also called the Caduceus, is two intertwined snakes in a perfect representation of the way our DNA coils. But what do the wings represent?

DNA does not fly, is it a coincidence that these wings also appear on the creator Gods, which are depicted in ancient Sumerian writings and Egyptian writings and images?

It could mean that the DNA symbol also represents its source, those who descended from heaven to Earth.

And this does not stop here, there is another point with which we can link all this.

In ancient Greece, the Caduceus represented Hermes, or later, the same god of the Romans called Mercury, and the commitments associated with that god. Those responsibilities were alchemy or the transformation of matter, trade, business, and death. So, is it also a coincidence that these were the responsibilities of the so-called Anunaki according to the ancient Sumerian tablets?

These tablets tell the story of the creator gods who descended from heaven to earth, genetically transforming the existing homo as the Neanderthal, for the purpose of their trade in order to serve theirrace. Again, a coincidence?

Evidence of a destroyed plant:

If the possibility of alien life seems highly unlikely, it is worth knowing a few things about our solar system and the odds that perhaps life existed here when other planets had uninhabitable environments. For example, in the 18th century, a German astronomer, Johann Tityus, discovered a mathematical pattern in the design of the planets and predicted the existence of another planet between Mars and Jupiter. Immediately astronomers sought to find it, but, instead of a planet, they found what appears to be pieces of one. This area is known today as the asteroid belt of our solar system. This hypothetical planet was named Phaethon, after the offspring of the sun god Helius from Greek mythology. Other legends claim that there was a planet called Maldek in our solar system, which was destroyed by its violent uninhabitability thousands of years ago. Legend has it that some of its inhabitants managed to escape and colonized Earth, so, appropriately enough, ¾ of our population are their descendants.

Evidence of nuclear destruction on Mars:

If Maldek was not a place for alien life, another planet could have been, and that could be Mars.

Recently, it has been published that Mars had vegetation and flowing water there is still water at the pole. However, NASA has long known that Mars has a high concentration of the isotope

Xenon-129 gas in its atmosphere. Xenon-129 is radioactive and does not occur naturally, as it is the result of a nuclear explosion. It was reported that in 1972 a nuclear reaction took place on Mars approximately 1.7 billion years ago. The head of the

U.S. Atomic Energy Commission, the late Dr. Glenn T. Seaborg, won a Nobel Prize for his work on the synthesis of heavy elements. This great scientist said that there is no way that a nuclear reaction could have happened naturally on Mars. So, if the reactions could not have been natural, did intelligent beings cause them?

This is already happening:

In case you still have any doubts, remember that this is already happening today. In other words, genetic manipulation is something we are doing.

Synthetic DNA made its first public appearance in 1967 and the last 50 years. Published discoveries are likely to be lagging years behind where technology has gone. You need only compare Morse code with a telephone, or the first camera with the Hubble telescope to see the speed at which technology has advanced in just a few decades. The truth is that we don't know what is happening behind closed doors with DNA manipulation.

Aliens in Earth's deepest lake

Although UFOs (unidentified flying objects) are very popular, the truth is that 50% of UFO encounters are connected with oceans and 15% more with lakes. This tells us something interesting: extraterrestrial beings tend to be more attached to water, although at this point, we must doubt the term "extraterrestrial" since there is a great possibility that, although there are intergalactic beings, there are also living intelligent species that we do not know living here on Earth, either underwater, under the Earth or among us.

I know that the title of what we will talk about here is quite shocking, but it is nothing compared to when you finish reading it.

This lake is no ordinary lake, as it is considered the largest freshwater body on the planet, containing 23% of the world's surface freshwater, more than all the great lakes of North America combined. This lake is not only the largest but also the deepest, with a depth of almost 2 kilometers. And to all this, let's add the age of the body of water, which scientists estimate to be at least 25 million years old, making it the oldest lake in the world. Globally, Lake Baikal's ecosystem is one of the richest in freshwater, and about 80% of the more than 3,700 species are found nowhere else in the world.

Given its mountainous location and unforgiving climate, it's easy to see why the lake's depths have never been fully explored. However, the mysteries and strange stories surrounding it are far more astounding still.

One of the first stories we will tell is that when a diving expedition was launched to survey the site and the deeper parts of the lake, the divers who joined the mission never expected to encounter what they found in the lake.

What did they see there?

The records revealed a story of seven divers who went into the lake to explore it. When they reached a depth of 50 meters, they all had a strange sensation, as they felt that someone or something was watching them and saw large shadows moving in the water. Suddenly, the divers would be confronted with the creepiest thing they had ever seen in their lives: in front of them were large aquatic humanoid beings, almost 3 meters tall. The strangest thing was that they were wearing some kind of gear, as they tell that they had tight-fitting silver suits and what appeared to be spherical helmets. And what did the Soviet divers do? The worst thing they could have done they tried to attack the beings to capture and investigate them later. The divers tried to throw a net over one of the beings, but at that very moment, all the divers were blown out of the water by an unknown powerful force. And since they were 50 meters deep in the lake, this sudden movement caused the divers to suffer from decompression sickness, which can be fatal.

The only way to save these men was to put them in pressure chambers, but what happened was that on that tragic day, the naval base only had a single chamber available and in working condition. Furthermore, these chambers could only take 2 people at a time. However, the mission commander forced 4 men into the pressure chamber, while the other 3, unable to enter the chamber, died on the beach. When the classified Soviet documents were released to the public, the Lake Baikal incident was reprinted in the pages of serious Russian socio-political publications, such as the Federation newspaper, which is a government media outlet.

Interestingly, no official denials were received about the event, and the defense ministry of what is now the Russian Federation left no comment.

But over the years, somehow, the declassified documents recounting this incident ended up disappearing and all that remained was this story they called "the Lake Baikal swimmers".

But we are not writing this just to tell you a story and nothing else, as you know, here we will go deep into each topic to connect some dots.

Many people have tried to refute what the divers claimed to

have seen, but the story you have just read has been supported by Alexey Tivanenko, a well-known doctor of historical sciences, and writer of more than 100 books and about 5000 articles on local history.

What Alexey Tivanenko did was to interview all the people near the lake and then write an article titled "Traces of real extraterrestrial life on Lake Baikal". In that article, he explained that almost all Baikal fishermen saw many strange occurrences on the lake over the years.

'I have hundreds of drawings with these 'Sons of Heaven',' said Alexey Tivanenko. Photo credits: NTV

Among his works, he tells a story told to him by one of the fishermen who saw the "silver swimmers". This man, as he tells, one night was fishing with some of his friends in a place near the Circum-Baikal railroad, on the south side of the lake. At this place, the lake breaks at a depth of almost 1400 meters immediately near the shore, so if you fall overboard death is assured because even in summer the temperature of the lake does not exceed 3 degrees Celsius. According to this man, around midnight while they were fishing in silence, they saw huge silver humanoid creatures begin to jump out of the icy waters of the lake as if they were playing a game. This man and his friends, upon seeing this, were terrified of what might happen to them, so they immediately threw down their nets and headed back to their village.

Now, we still have to mention a few more things that happened in this mysterious lake. Let's go back to the present day, specifically to 2015, when "The Siberian Times" published an article titled "Aliens and UFOs in the world's deepest lake", in which it showed this incredible photo you are seeing here below of the cigar-shaped objects flying over the lake.

At this point, we could already begin to suppose that in this lake there could be secret bases operating from the depths where beings exist that we have no idea about, but that thousands of locals and visitors to the lake have seen over the years.

Now, how would it be possible for flying ships to leave the lake if in winter the lake freezes completely and the thickness of theice reaches 2 meters, completely sealing the lake? To answer this we will delve into the latest lake-related mystery we will see here, which was first discovered in 2009 when astronauts abroad on the international space station noticed two mysterious holes in the thick ice of Lake Baikal.

Apparently, every year when the lake freezes over, mysterious circular holes appear in different places in the ice, as if something is coming out or going into the lake breaking through the 2 meter thick ice. These circles last from days to months until cold weather freezes the circles again. These circles were so large that they could only be seen from airplanes or satellites, so scientists tried to solve this strange mystery, and an international team of researchers from France, Russia and Mongolia was set up to study the ice rings in 2010.
Among their conclusions, they drew 3 theories:

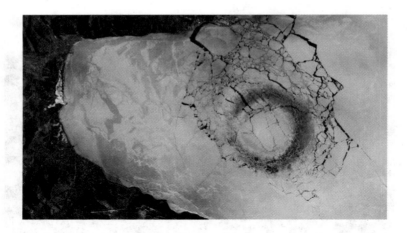

The circles were caused by warmer water rising in the lake, but the problem with this theory is that some of the circles were located in the deepest parts of the lake with the coldest water, so it did not end up being viable.

Methane gas bubbles from the deep lake bottom caused the circles. This theory was also not viable since some of these ice circles also appeared in the shallower water, areas with no possible gas emissions.

So the question is, what or who created these strange shapes in the ice?

The truth is that to this day there is no explanation for this or for anything else that happens in Lake Baikal, but like any truth, it always becomes visible to the eyes of those who are prepared to recognize it.

The truth is that for the moment we have no official information to confirm what is down there, but the historical facts bring us very close to what seems to exist in the depths of this lake and any other ocean on the planet.

Again, at this point it is more difficult to prove that this is not true, since the evidence far outweighs any kind of rational explanation that anyone can come up with.

This giant pyramid changes the entire history of mankind

Let's continue going to the root of all this. A few years ago, what is so far considered the oldest pyramid in the world was discovered, much older than the civilization of Egypt and Sumer. A pyramid that is clear proof that an intelligent civilization existed long before the Ice Age.

But reaching this conclusion did not happen overnight.

It all goes back to the year 1914 when one of the settlers heard the story that in the jungle there was a lost palace that was built by mystical kings long ago. This person soon found something incredible, as he found a huge hill with what appeared to have some sort of steps leading to its top. At the top of these steps, he found a large collection of rectangular blocks scattered in all directions. Had he stumbled upon the mysterious palace? Well, he quickly sent a letter to the Dutch government to request a professional expedition to explore the site further. After the story began to be told, a great interest in this place was generated, but the Dutch government never sent an expedition to investigate the site further, until, in 1940, Indonesia gained full independence from Holland, but the site had already been forgotten.

Fortunately for all mystery seekers, in 1979, three residents of Java rediscovered the site while wandering through the jungle. These three immediately reported the find to local officials, who identified the site as a lost hill called Gunung Padang. In just a few weeks, the Indonesian government sent teams from the Directorate of Heritage Protection and Management and the National Archaeology Center to further explore the site.

Shortly thereafter, researchers mapped the site and began to document its archaeological features.

First, the stone blocks, which the Irish settlers had encountered all those years before, of which there were almost an infinite number of them, about 10 feet long and weighing more than 249 kilos. Some of them even weighed more than 589 kilos.

The researchers realized that these blocks were not made by humans, but were a naturally formed andesite rock forged by a volcano, which meant that someone had transported them to the top of the hill some 90 meters above the valley below.

While they were investigating, they discovered that the blocks were not randomly scattered, as you see in the image, they were organized in rectangular stone enclosures and rock mounds.

Whoever put them up there using the blocks for construction. It looked like five separate terraces covered the hill, in an area of 914 square meters and all linked by an ascending staircase of 370 steps.

Instead of using radiocarbon detention to detect the age of the site, the researchers used simple guesses, estimating that it was built somewhere between 2500 and 1500 B.C. by measuring the chips in the blocks.

For this reason, as interesting as the site was, it was nothing transcendental, since it was just another one of the simple settlements no more different from so many others found around the world.

And so, it was believed that Gunung Padang was, until 2011...

Danny Hilman Nata Villager, a senior geologist at the Indonesian Institute of Science, came across something surprising: the Gunung Padang Hill.

What caught his attention was the peculiar shape of the hill, in his words:

"It's not like the surrounding topography, which is very eroded, this looks very young. It looked artificial."

In 2011, Nata Villager followed his curious instinct when he was chosen to lead a team of geologists from the Institute of Science with archaeologists from the University of Indonesia on a government-sponsored project that examined the site.

At first, the finds obtained were unremarkable, as initial radiocarbon dating performed on soils below the stone blocks yielded dates of 1500 to 400 B.C., very similar to the initial estimate made in 1979.

But not everything was left there, because as they began to dig deeper, the dates began to date thousands of years before Christ.

Using tube drills that extracted cores of soil and stone, they obtained evidence of numerous human-made sculptures found beneath the surface. What was most surprising was that the deeper they went, the older the material they unearthed.

Below the surface, the researchers found three distinct layers.

The first was only 2500 to 3500 years old. The second, at 3 meters below the surface, dates from 7500 to 8300 BC.

The third, at a depth of almost 15 meters, was about 28,000 years old.

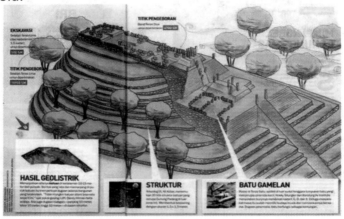

Think how incredible this is, because even at 7500 years old this would already put the civilization that inhabited this pyramid at about 3500 years before the ancient Sumerians, and 4500 years before the ancient Egyptians. And as if that were not enough, the information obtained from 28,000 years old was something never seen before that would completely revolutionize the history of mankind and everything we know about the ancient civilizations that inhabited the earth.

But all this did not stop there, as the researchers went deeper and found another arrangement of rectangular blocks organized in a matrix structure, in the second layer.

While in the third layer, they found additional rock structures that included, what appeared to be, large subway structures, cavities, and chambers.

All of this was published in a report on their findings, stating that:

"Our studies prove that the structure does not cover only the upper part, but also envelops the slopes covering an area of approximately 15 hectares at least. The structures are not only superficial but are rooted to a greater depth. Their exposure clearly shows that the younger construction is built on top of an older, more sophisticated layer of cultural rock."

In other words, Gunung Padang was not just a hill at all, but a huge step pyramid-built thousands of years ago in the past.

Well, if this was possible, who built such constructions in the past if human civilization supposedly began officially many years later?

Nata Villager thought she had the answer:

"The geophysical evidence is unequivocal, Gunung Padang is not a natural hill, but a man-made pyramid, and the origins of the construction here, go back long before the last ice age. Since the work is massive even at the deepest levels and testifies to the kinds of sophisticated construction skills that were deployed to build the pyramids of Egypt or the largest megalithic sites in Europe, I can only conclude that we are looking at the work of a lost civilization. It's crazy, but it's data."

At the time and seeing the potential this discovery had for the country, the Indonesian government immediately jumped on board, investing a lot of money in the project and giving the researchers state-of-the-art equipment, as well as calling in the Indonesian military to help with the excavation.

The country's president called the work at Gunung Padang an important asset to humanity and even had a helipad built on top of the hill so he could visit and see the progress for himself, but it wasn't all a fairy tale for Nata Villager and her team.

Because his invention was so innovative, it eventually became the subject of much controversy as history was being rewritten.

Almost immediately and without much reason, the

archaeological establishment in Indonesia lined up in opposition, leading to pressure on the political authorities and local agitation demanding that the project be stopped.

What they were saying was that proper excavation procedures were not being followed and that the results were built on biased conclusions, as well as complaining about the large budget that had been devoted to the project, claiming that they needed the money for their more important work.

But as the truth always comes out, as time went by it became clear the main reason why they were so opposed to this discovery.

Despite having conducted no research of its own, the archaeological establishment claimed that it knew that the remains at Gunung Padang could not be more than 5000 years old, simply because it was illogical to suggest that a civilization existed in such a distant past. It could not be possible, because if it were it would defy the records of human civilization contained within the history books.

In other words, their real problem was that they were unwilling to change their way of thinking, being unable to consider that what they knew about human history might be wrong.

Despite the powerful imposition, the Indonesian government agreed to further research, so they continued for a while longer with government support.

On that last trek, the discoveries were even more astonishing, for as they cleared more of the jungle to continue the expeditions, they uncovered numerous relics throughout the area: jewelry and pottery, tools and household items, weapons, and even never-before-seen coins dating back to 5200 BC, which was an astonishing date since modern science insisted that the world's first coins appeared around 600 BC. In addition, they discovered that the cement mixture they used to hold the giant blocks of Gunung Padang together was composed of clay, silicon, and iron, suggesting that iron smelting technology was known many thousands of years in the past, which was also impossible for conventional science as they claimed that the iron age did not begin until 1201 BC.

But there was more... as they continued their work, another group of scientists arrived determined to find something else they had heard about.

As the local legend of Gunung Padang said that the blocks emit mysterious energy, they decided to investigate them. The researchers discovered that the blocks emitted a relatively high frequency, at levels corresponding to the standard Western musical scale, and as Nikola Tesla said:

"If you want to understand the secrets of the universe, think in terms of energy, frequency, and vibration."

At this point, Gunung Padang not only appeared to be proof of an extremely ancient civilization but also of, as Nata Villager put it, "proof of an intelligent and extremely advanced civilization."

Well, the discoveries finally came to an end, when in 2014 a new ruler of Indonesia was elected, and, unlike his predecessor, he sided with the archaeological establishment on the issue of Gunung Padang. Thus, on October 1, 2014, the investigation at the site was stopped altogether, and to this day there is still Joko Widodo as president.

As it has not been possible to continue with the investigations, the mysteries were left in the middle, and for the moment it is not known who the inhabitants of this civilization were, but 3 things are very clear:

1. History must be rewritten and what is told today in books is not true.
2. There are many more mysteries of which we haveno idea.
3. Gunung Padang is clear evidence of an ancient, intelligent civilization that existed here on Earth.

Leaving this on the table, we will soon move on to chapter two to talk about the control of humanity, but first it is necessary to go to the root. Let's look into a theory that has a lot of traction today.

Our planet could be a cosmic prison

This is a theory that carries quite a lot of weight since the coincidences that support it are overwhelming.
For example, humans are the only beings on Earth with a tendency to tan easily, with an aversion to natural foods, and with high rates of chronic diseases and extremely high infant mortality rates. And if we were born here, Earth should be the perfect place for us, but then why do these things happen to us?

Dr. Ellis Silver discusses this topic in depth in his book "Humans are not from Earth, a scientific assessment of the evidence".
In the book, Silver explains that humans are aliens, as the evidence suggests, considering how humans have adapted to the industrial environment. Silver also includes, during an interview with Yahoo News, "There is a prevalent feeling among many people in which they feel that they don't belong here or that something just isn't right."
But then, for what reason were we sent to Earth? According to Ellis, the violent nature of the human race is the answer. "Until humans learn to act in a primal state, we are somehow doomed to eternity on this prison planet and will never be able to return home."
What supports these observations made by Dr. Silver? Most of his readings are based on selective readings about species differences. For example, he compares humans to lizards because of their ability to stay in the sun without getting sunburned. Silver believes that the reason why humans get sunburned is that we are not native to this planet and were

simply brought here. Other contradictory evidence is the 99% similarity between chimpanzees and humans in their genetic makeup. That fact suggests that we share an evolutionary history that goes back 5 to 6 million years. But according to Dr. Bernard Hubble, a bioinformatician at the Marx Planck Institute, Earth's inhabitants have common metabolism and genetics, and this suggests that most probably once upon a time, there was a universal ancestor and that all living things are related to each other.

Ultimately, Silver's theory is very much related to the biblical idea that we were put here and that we must behave in harmony to ascend to heaven, and therefore we are in a kind of "prison". But if we get out of that idea we can see certain similarities that suggest the fact that since the beginning there has been intervention by "beings" from another dimension with another type of intelligence that inhabited the Earth.

Add to this the fact that there are planets out there very similar to Earth and that there is a possibility that life could not have been created by selection scattered throughout the universe, and we could summarize that, if there is life here, there is life elsewhere.

Let us then move on to answer another big question: do we live in a simulated reality?

We live in a huge video game programmed by beings much more advanced than us.

I could begin these lines by saying that shortly, it will be difficult to distinguish reality from fiction since technological advances are increasing very fast, but the truth is that this near future is the one we are living in now. Technology is already capable of approaching almost perfection in scenographies and human details to capture us in video games or the metaverse.

Since the hypothesis has always been about what would happen when this happens, I believe we are about to enter into living the answer to that question.

Well, if humans reach the point of creating technology that is capable of matching what we believe to be a reality, there is also the possibility that more technologically advanced beings can also do so, and are doing so.

If we consider in turn the fact that these beings could have knowledge millions of times superior to ours in terms of development and consciousness, there is the possibility that we are living in their creation, that is, in their own "video game". How can we know that we are not already in a simulation?

Although I like to ask questions to get an answer, the truth is that there is no way to verify that we are not in a simulation, being very feasible the possibility that we are in one.

Could all of our reality be virtual? According to ancient wisdom, yes.

The theory that reality is not real goes back thousands of years. For example, in the Tao, a mysterious luminous unity, underlying and sustaining all things, Yin and Yang, is described.

In Hinduism, the word "Maya" means unreal or delusion.

In the words of Yoga Vasistha:

"The world is but a mere vibration of consciousness in space. It seems to exist even as a goblin seems to exist before the eyes of the ignorant, but all this is Maya. For here there is no contradiction between infinite consciousness and the apparent existence of the universe. It is like the wonderful dream of a person who is awake."

An author named Don Miguel Ruiz who shares about Toltec wisdom, an ancient Mexican culture, said the following:

"The Toltecs believed that life is a dream and that we are

always dreaming, even when we are awake. It is as if we are starring in our movie, and following a script, we write ourselves. Everyone around us is starring in their movie based on their concepts of the world."

In 1989, physicist John Archibald Wheeler suggested that the Universe is fundamentally mathematical and can be considered to emerge from the information. He coined the famous aphorism "it from bit".

Years later, in 2003, philosopher Nick Bostrom, of Oxford University, formulated his simulation hypothesis, which holds that it is very likely that we live in a reality controlled by a mastermind. Bostrom argues in his theory that there are one or more civilizations so advanced that they are capable of creating simulations indistinguishable from reality, where the participants would be unaware that they are in a simulation. And of course, we would be those characters in the simulation, just as in the Sims game. Bostrom also argues that since we are in the creation of computer simulations, one of the following results concerning it must be true:

1. Humans will become extinct before they can run simulations
2. Humans of the future will decide, for whatever reason, not to continue developing simulation
3. We are all living in a computer simulation

Adding more scientists' comments to this theory, Seth Lloyd, a physicist at the Massachusetts Institute of Technology, suggests that the entire Universe could be a giant quantum computer. Lloyd says that our physical reality could be a simulated virtual reality rather than an objective world that exists independently of the observer. The American physicist has devoted himself to making analogies between our objective world and the way computers used to work. In this way, he has given support to the idea that we live in a kind of reality governed by a mind that we can neither identify nor describe.

Any virtual reality world will be based on information processing. Ultimately, everything is digitized or pixelated down to a minimum size that cannot be further subdivided: bits (hence the phrase).

Similarly, elementary particles, which constitute all visible matter in the Universe, are the smallest units of matter. In short, Lloyd claims that our world is pixelated. The laws of physics that govern the Universe also resemble lines of code in a computer that would follow a simulation in running the program. On the other hand, mathematical equations, numbers, and geometric patterns are present everywhere.

Another physics curiosity that supports Lloyd's simulated reality hypothesis is the maximum speed limit in our Universe: the speed of light. In virtual reality, this limit would correspond to the speed limit of the processor.

And well, going now to quantum mechanics, it suggests that nature is not "real", since particles in particular states, such as specific locations, do not appear to exist unless they are observed or measured. Similarly, virtual reality needs an observer or programmer to make things happen. Lloyd's ideas go hand in hand with what is theorized by so-called information physics, which suggests that space-time and matter are not fundamental phenomena. Instead, physical reality is fundamentally composed of bits of information, from which our experience of space-time arises.

But how to demonstrate that reality is indeed subject to a large amount of information provided by a computer?

Melvin M. Vopson, a researcher at the University of Portsmouth, claims that information is another form of matter in the Universe. He has even calculated the expected information content per elementary particle. Vopson proposes that to prove that Lloyd's theories are true, one can erase the information contained inside elementary particles by letting them and their antiparticles annihilate in a flash of energy, emitting "photons," or particles of light.

When we come to understand the consciousness of reality we see that it is only information, and we are generating a perception of our consciousness.

For example, your eyes receive light, your ears receive sound, and it's all information.

These electrical impulses end up in neural patterns, but if you were in a dark cave, your brain could still receive the same pattern of neural stimulation. How? Through your imagination, perception is generated inside the brain, not outside of it. No one experiences the same reality as we all receive and express different information, and in turn, we are all part of that larger unified consciousness. Kind of like separate constructs in a unified field.

And what is the point of all this?

Just as the objective of a virtual game which is to win by experiencing challenges that are then overcome, this reality would help us evolve as we experience relationships with others of our free will.

This virtual physical reality is our school, and we are characters evolving in consciousness through an information system.

"Everything that is an anomaly makes sense if you realize you are creating it."

If you learn not to judge and master your belief system, even suffering then becomes something that helps you evolve. If this is all a simulation and this is the reality, you have created this book, every word you are reading, and the only truth.

This might seem like a hallucination, but it all becomes clear when you observe that your very belief system is the clear confirmation that you are creating the world from within yourself.

And what do all that we have seen here have in common? They have in common the truth, which becomes evident to those who are ready to receive it and to those who dare to leave their limited beliefs behind.

At this point, I must remind you that this book is just getting started, as we have not even revealed 1% of all the information you will be entering once you advance into the following pages, as I suggest you continue to remember that you know nothing, that this book has no truth to it, and that whatever you need to know for your evolution is what will be presented to you here.

Now, let's move on to chapter two, the control of humanity.

CONTROL OF HUMANITY

People who are reading this book probably already know that the greatest mass control is exercised daily through the media. Today, TV is still the place where most people watch the news of what is happening in the world and where the most drama is usually exercised. Although unfortunately, this virus is now spreading to other social networks, and wherever you are and whatever you do, you will come across some dramatic news, and if it is something that affects a group of people en masse or all of humanity, all the more reason.

I will be more specific so we can go much deeper into the subject.

What do I mean when I say "virus" in the previous paragraph?

In that, the greatest weapon of manipulation exercised by the "great ones" (we will also call them the elite) is fear. Through fear, uncertainty, and repetition, they end up establishing in our minds thoughts related to "the world is in chaos", "we are all going to die", "people are dying for X reason", "the third world war is coming", etc.

And of course, not only that. This is when something massive happens (which makes the manipulation evident), but during the rest of the year or in the time when there is nothing new to tell/invent about something like that, the only thing they show in the news are robberies, deaths, accidents, or new diseases that appear.

But you know, I don't blame them, I don't think anyone is to blame for anything. But I do believe in one word: responsibility.

I believe that both you and I are responsible not for what we show on the news, but for what we choose to consume.

Or why do you think all they show is that kind of stuff? Because that's what people love to consume! Watching that generates a certain addiction and curiosity. It may be for reasons like: "not to miss what's going on", "to be informed" or whatever you want. But the truth is that it is simply addictive for your mind. It is even funny to see how they play with colors and use red (understood as a danger to your mind) to draw even more attention so that we can't take our eyes off the TV.

Besides, let's be honest, with how globalized the world is, spreading the rumor that there is a new disease or that the third world war is coming and then you and I will be scared shitless is something very simple. Just pick up the phone and tell them to publish something like that to all the puppets they have as ringleaders to the public.

But why would they do such a thing? The answer is simple and we have already given it, for control.

It is easier to do things if they have millions of people up their sleeves and thinking the same way without questioning anything.

It is easy to rule as you please with your rules if no one questions, even a little, the veracity of every act. What you have just read is not a criticism, far from it. It is also not venting on my part toward this massive control. It is simply a fact and from my reality what I see. But it does not have to be true.

Anyway, I consider it useful to be able to get deeper and deeper into this book and build that one truth. You haven't seen anything yet, I haven't asked you much yet. But keep your mind strapped in if you don't want it to be blown away in the next few pages. As a phrase goes: "He who controls the media, controls the minds".

What would you tell me if the biggest epidemics and pandemics in history were planned? Of course, even COVID. And I highlight this now (even though it is the subject of the next chapter) because the virus that has been going around for two years is a clear example of this control through fear that I am mentioning to you. Since its appearance, the news and social networks were the only thing they talked about. And if all you read and hear about is that thousands of people are dying from this disease, aren't you a little afraid of getting sick?

That's why the real virus is fear!

All this allows me to show you something that will leave you with your mouth open: The Economist magazine.

One of the most influential media in the world is The Economist, a weekly publication based in London, which frequently covers current international relations and the state of the economy from a global point of view.

The first issue of the weekly saw the light of day in September 1843 under the editorship of James Wilson and today the leading publication is owned by the powerful conglomerate The Economist Group, a publishing company 50% controlled by the Rothschild and Agnelli families.

Although we will not talk here about the wealthiest families in the world (we did that in the book Satseupser) it is worth remembering that the Rothschilds are the largest banking family in the world to whom all the credit money is owed. So, yes, it is one of the most powerful families today, which also means that it is one of the most controlling.

The covers that predict the future of humanity

If you analyze the covers of the different editions of The Economist magazine, you can see how, likecryptography, they transmit hidden messages thatend up being a kind of prediction of where the worldis heading.

This is the magazine for this year 2022:

Let's take a closer look at their predictions:

1. **Democracy versus autocracy.** The U.S. midterm elections and China's Communist Party congress will vividly contrast their rival political systems. Which is better at delivering stability, growth and innovation? This rivalry will play out in everything from trade to technology regulation, from vaccines to space stations. As President Joe Biden attempts to unite the free world under the banner of democracy, his dysfunctional and divided country is a bad advertisement on its merits.

2. **Pandemic to endemic.** New antiviral pills, improved antibody treatments and more vaccines are coming. For vaccinated people in the developed world, the virus will no longer be life-threatening. But it will still pose a deadly danger in the developing world. Unless vaccines can be scaled up, Covid-19 will have become one of many endemic diseases that affect the poor but not the rich.

3. **Inflation concerns.** Supply chain disruptions and increased demand for energy have pushed up prices. Central bankers say it is temporary, but not everyone believes them. Britain is at particular risk of stagflation, due to post-Brexit labor shortages and its reliance on expensive natural gas.

4. **The future of work.** There is a broad consensus that the future is "hybrid" and that more people will spend more days working from home. But there is plenty of room for disagreement about the details - how many days and which ones, and will it be fair? Surveys show that women have less desire to return to the office, so they may be at risk of being passed over for promotions. Also looming are debates over tax rules and remote monitoring of workers.

5. **The new *techlash*.** Regulators in the U.S. and Europe have been trying to rein in tech giants for years, but have yet to make a dent in their growth or profits. Now China has taken the lead, targeting its tech companies in a brutal crackdown. President Xi Jinping wants them to focus on "deep tech" that provides geostrategic advantage, not on frivolities like gaming and shopping. But will this boost Chinese innovation or stifle industry dynamism?

6. **Cryptocurrency is growing.** Like all disruptive technologies, cryptocurrencies are being tamed as regulators tighten the rules. Central banks are also looking to launch their own centralized digital currencies. The result is a three-way fightfor the future of finance, between the crypto- blockchain-DeFi crowd, more traditional tech companies and central banks, that will intensify in 2022.

7. **Climate crisis.** As wildfires, heat waves and floods increase in frequency, a surprising lack of urgency prevails among policymakers when it comes to addressing climate change. Moreover, decarbonization requires the West and China tocooperate, just as their geopolitical rivalry deepens. Pay attention to a solar engineering experiment that Harvard researchers will conduct in 2022, releasing dust from a balloon at high altitude, a technique that, at this rate, may be needed to buy the world more time to decarbonize.

8. **Travel issues** Activity is picking up as economies reopen. But countries that followed a zero covid "suppression" strategy, such as Australia and New Zealand, face the difficult task of managing the transition to a world where the virus is endemic. Meanwhile, nearly half of all business travel is gone for good. That's good for the planet, but bad for tourists whose travel is subsidized by business travelers who spend money.

9. **Space careers.** 2022 will be the first year in which more people go into space as paying passengers than government employees, transported by rival space tourism companies. China will complete its new space station. Filmmakers are competing to make movies in

microgravity. And NASA will crash a space probe into an asteroid, in a real-life mission that sounds like a Hollywood movie.

10.   **Political balls.** The Winter Olympics in Beijing and the World Cup in Qatar will be reminders of how sport can unite the world, but also of how major sporting events often end up as political balls. Protests directed at both host countries are expected, although boycotts of national teams seem unlikely.

Also, something very clear that we can find is the logo of the Cardano, Ethereum, Litecoin and Bitcoin cryptocurrencies perhaps referring that these cryptocurrencies are the imminent future towards which we are heading.

For those of you who are more curious, I suggest you enter "The Economist Predictions Magazine" in the YouTube search engine and then enter the year you want to see. There you have hours of content of people analyzing each of the magazines and, as there are many from previous years, you will be able to see how the things that each magazine wrote about have come true.

And while we're on the subject of predictions... how many are familiar with The Simpsons series?

In the world of conspiracies this TV series has become very popular because of the incredible "coincidences" that occur in terms of events that happen in the series and then end up happening in reality.

Let's take a look at some of the most famous predictions this TV series has made that have come true:

The great secret of the Simpsons

9/11

When Lisa shows Bart a poster, it shows the message that the number 9 and the two towers form the date of September 11, predicting the attack 4 years earlier. After the attack, the episode was withdrawn, but since 2017 it started to be rebroadcast.

The presidency of Donald Trump

In the famous episode "Bart to the Future," Lisa Simpson is president, which is not terribly difficult tounderstand. But what is strange is that this episode,aired in 2000, predicted that she would succeedPresident Donald Trump.

Tiger attack

In episode 91 of season 5, Springfield, out comes the attack of a tiger on one of its tamers, Roy. This aired on December 16, 1993 and a decade later it actually happened in a Las Vegas show, with the real Roy as the main character.

Richard Branson's journey into space

No, they didn't call him Richard Branson by name, but even Virgin Atlantic realized that a 2008 episode of a billionaire in space looked remarkably like Richard Branson, who got on a plane in 2021 (for real) and headed into the stratosphere, reaching 85 kilometers high and floating with a crew of Virgin employees.

The 2014 World Cup

   In episode 546 of season 25, You Don't Have to Be a Referee, the Simpsons predicted three relevant events of the World Cup in Brazil, three months before they happened. The first was Neymar's injury, which sidelined him from the competition. The second, Colombia's passage to the round of 16 and the last, the semifinal between Germany and Brazil in which the home team lost 7-1.

Video calls and virtual reality

   As Lisa and Bart grow older, the whole Simpsons' environment is nourished by new technologies, which at that time were not as widespread as they are now. In episode 122 of season 6, Lisa's Wedding, aired in 1995, we see how Lisa, who lives in England, contacts Marge by video call. On the other hand, Bart introduces virtual reality games in the episode Bart of the Future, released on March 19, 2000, 15 years before their use became widespread.

Virus

The Simpsons predicted some of the viruses that most affected the world's population in recent years: Ebola and the coronavirus. In the 1997 episode Lisa's Saxophone, Marge shows Bart a book with a person bedridden with Ebola on the cover; years later, this virus unleashed a dangerous pandemic in Liberia. On the other hand, although they did not predict the coronavirus, in the chapter Marge in prison of 1993, it was seen how a virus arrived from China in a package that Homer had ordered and how this disease affected the whole world.

January 2021

The last prediction was in January 2021 in which one of the new episodes of season 32 saw Marge and several Springfield neighbors wearing masks.

As we can see, many predictions have been made. And of course, reflecting on it would make us create hundreds of doubts and theories about it.

In reality, whether we want to believe it or not, it is something that is happening and has been happening for years. The Simpsons is somehow predicting the future, or perhaps, creating it.

We cannot rule out that millions of people have been influenced by this television series. I mean that, from a more quantum level where we are all connected and information is all one, it is not unreasonable to conclude that everything already exists. And if everything already exists, it means that both the past and the future we are living now. Therefore, there would be no past or future, but simply an infinite sea of possibilities where we as humans can choose some and enter that reality. And how is it possible that things happen globally that seem like predictions? Perhaps, because under the influence of this TV series, there are millions of people creating the same reality. In other words: accessing the same quantum information.

A "simple" board game that knows what's going to happen

And in addition to these predictions, we cannot miss the Illuminati Letters. Although again about these letters you have much more information in the book Satseupser, let's see some others or those that agree with the predictions that have also been made by The Simpsons.

Before we get into the subject, let's get a little context. In 1994, Steve Jackson invented a role- playing game called the "Illuminati New World Order" game. What was the purpose of the game or what is it about?

The game consists of developing and consolidating a power structure through which you can rule the world from the shadows in the name of your chosen order, while manipulating society and dealing apocalyptic blows to your opponents. Interesting and... fun?

Also, it is important that we keep the date of creation, since the shocking and fascinating thing about this is that the game was created long before the predictions were fulfilled.

This game has become popular in the mystery community for its shocking predictions, among them the September 11 attack and the COVID pandemic, among others that we will see. Some say that this is evidence enough of the control they exert without us realizing it and how everything is basically planned by this Illuminati sect or who knows what they call themselves today.

Letters 1 and 2: Epidemic and disease control.

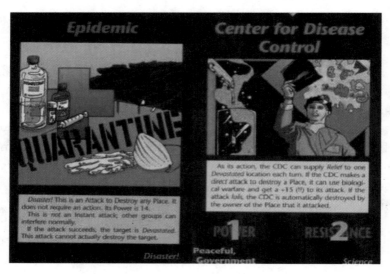

Card 1: Epidemic

This is what the description of the card says: *Disaster! This is an attack to destroy any location. It does not require an action ...*

This is not an instant attack, other groups can interfere normally. If the attack is successful, the target will be devastated.

This attack cannot actually destroy the target.

On this occasion, this letter called "Epidemic" shows in the image the word quarantine, a mask, gloves and disinfectants. Was the coronavirus planned by the illuminati?

It is curious to observe how this letter represents in such a specific way what we have been living for two years now. Quarantine, masks and a flu called COVID.

Card 2: Disease control

Here's what it says in the description: *As an action, the CDC* (acronym for Center for Disease Control) *can provide relief to one devastated site at a time. If the CDC makes a direct attack to destroy a site, it can usebiological warfare and get +15 to the attack. If the attack fails, the CDC will automatically be destroyed by the owner of the attacked location.*

This may refer to the theories that accompanied COVID in its early days related to the tension between the US and China. When the virus broke out, the stock market (where the world's largest companies are listed) had the biggest drop in history. As we will see in the next letter, everything may be revolving around market manipulation and thepurpose may be nothing more than economic. In fact, if anywhere it is evident that the greatest control is exercised, it is through the monetary system.

Card 3: Market manipulation

This is what it says in the description: *This card can be used at any time.....*

And the truth is that they use it, at any time and without the most advance warning, of course. Neither you nor I will be able to know exactly when the next world collapse or the next time the economy will be affected. It so happens that when it happens it is always due to some external factor which is surrounded by mysticism and theories.

Let's see, I am not saying that it is not natural for the stock market to fall, what I am trying to show you is how obvious it is that they manipulate it to seek their own benefit. What all this hides behind is spreading fear, the biggest virus.

From my point of view, how this works is very simple:

First they start planning the economy and then they destroy it so that people panic and accept more easily the new rules of the New World Order. Something like... create a virus, generate fear through the media, then create the solution (vaccine) and be the hero of the show.

Card 4: Mask of death

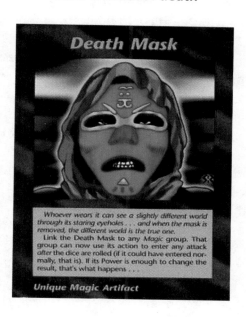

Whoever wears it can see a slightly different world through their eyes ... and when the mask is removed, the different world is the real one.

This letter does not directly contain a prediction or another conspiracy theory, but it does give me room to cover a little more of what this book is about and what I am showing you here.

When you take off the mask or the blindfold you were wearing, you begin to see things that others don't see, or things that were always there but that you couldn't see before because maybe you didn't even imagine they existed.

The card, in my opinion, is called "death mask" because while we wear it we are conditioned to the "truths" that have been sold to us as true, but once we take it off, we can access the infinite world of possibilities. Also, within this, I think it is evident that it is called "death" because in the 3D physical world we live in, death is a fact, when in reality it is not so at a metaphysical level. Death could be nothing more than a social construction? Is that, if we are energy and all of it is... how could anything die? Well though, the real question and the one that intrigues me the most to ask you is... would you be willing to take off your mask?

You may think it's ridiculous for me to ask since if you're reading this book it's because you're not afraid of anything, least of all knowing the truth. But I would like you to really feel that question. If all this that you will see here, at least one thousandth of it could be true, how would you feel?

Out there they say there are some things that are better left unknown. I agree. But I also believe that we deserve to know absolutely everything and that all of it will come to the extent that one is willing to receive it. To the extent that one is that, connects
with that and serves you for this passage through this dimension that you are now experiencing.

Finally, appreciate for yourself this letter and its comparison with a very important historical event. The September 11 attacks.

Cards 5 and 6: Terrorist Nuclear Bomb andPentagon

A lot of things have been said about the Twin Towersattack and many of them have been labeled as crazyand even stupid. One of them is the fact that the twintowers were not destroyed by an airplane, but weredemolished by explosives from inside the tower. Thisis based on the fact that it seems a bit unlikely that the steel beams were brought down simply by the fuel from the planes and their explosion, even takinginto account that the alleged crash occurred at the heights of the 47th floor.

In addition to this, we have the illuminati card you are looking at on your left which is entitled "Terrosit Nuke" i.e. "Terrorist Nuclear Bomb".

And let's remember, these letters were created 6 years

before the attack.

As if that weren't enough, there's even more.

Some have said that the media was part of the conspiracy since they supposedly knew every single thing   that   was going   to   happen. It is said that the main channels had a script and to back this up, there is a video of Jane Standley, a BBC journalist, in which she is seen reporting the events against the backdrop of the fire in the towers.

Between broadcasts, a banner appeared in the middle of their report indicating that 7 World Trade Center had also collapsed. The text lasted more than a minute on screen. However, by that time the building had not collapsed. It fell minutes later.

Card 6: Pentagon

Well, the other image below the twin towers is none other than the Pentagon, which also suffered an alleged terrorist attack that same day. Although there are not many theories about it since the main focus of attention was on the twin towers, I am enclosing that letter and the respective real image to further reaffirm the same. The illuminati charts predicted these events in detail. Although, let me correct, the only thing these letters did was to tell us in advance something that was planned. Something that the entire population did not know was going to happen, but for some people it was already written. Finally, and to close this chapter, I want us to look at something.

Overwhelming evidence on the elite's plan and ultra-advanced technology

At this point I know that the information we have seen so far is mostly shocking, but I saved a little more for last. Did you know that there are patents registered not only for diseases but also for "extraterrestrial" technology?

Well, when someone creates something and wants to own it, they have to patent it. And many of these patents appear on Google and are publicly available. So, let's see what some of them have to say:

Before we continue, if you want to see the same thing I will show you here, just type the patent code in the Google search engine.

Patent N°1: Coronavirus

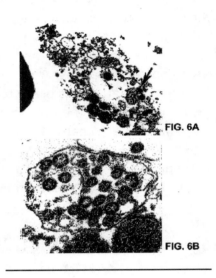

FIG. 6A

FIG. 6B

Code: US7220852B1

This is what it says on Google:

A newly isolated human coronavirus (SARS-CoV), the causative agent of severe acute respiratory syndrome (SARS), is disclosed herein. Also provided are the nucleic acid sequence of the SARS-CoV genome and amino acid sequences of SARS-CoV open reading frames, as well as methods for using these molecules to detect a SARS-CoV and detect infections with SARS-CoV. Immunostimulatory compositions are also provided, along with methods for their use.

Patent N°2: Triangular Spacecraft

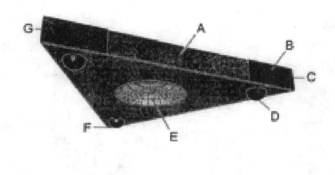

Code: US20060145019A1

This is what it says on Google:

A spacecraft that has a triangular hull with vertical electrostatic linear charges at each corner that produce a horizontal electric field parallel to the sides of the hull. This field, interacting with a plane wave emitted by antennas on the side of the hull, generates a force per volume that combines lift and propulsion.

Patent N°3: A full body teleportation system?

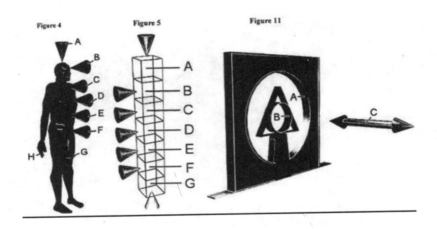

Code: US20060071122A1

This is what it says on Google:

A pulsed gravitational wave wormhole generator system that teleports a human being through hyperspace from one location to another.

Patent N°4: Manipulation of the nervous systemby electromagnetic fields from monitors.

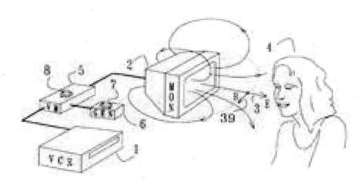

Code: US6506148B2

This is what it says on Google:

Physiological effects have been observed in a humansubject in response to stimulation of the skin with weak electromagnetic fields pulsed with certain frequencies near ½ Hz or 2.4 Hz, such as to excite a sensory resonance. Many computers monitors and TV tubes, when displaying pulsed images, emit pulsed electromagnetic fields of sufficient amplitude to cause such excitation. Thus, it is possible to manipulate a subject's nervous system by pulsing images displayed on a nearby computer monitor or TV set. For the latter, the pulsed image can be embedded in the program material, or it can be superimposed by modulating a video stream, either as an RF signal or as a video signal. The image displayed on a computer monitor can be effectively pulsed by a simple computer program.

Patent No. 5: Electric dipole spacecraft

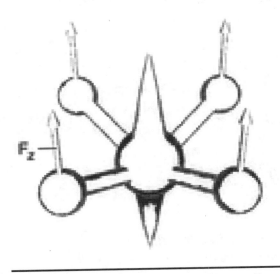

Code: US20060038081A1

This is what it says on Google:

This invention is a rotating spacecraft that produces an electric dipole in four rotating sphericalconducting domes that perturb a uniform spherical electric field to create a magnetic moment that interacts with the gradient of a magnetic field that generates a lift force on the hull.

Patent N°6: Ebola

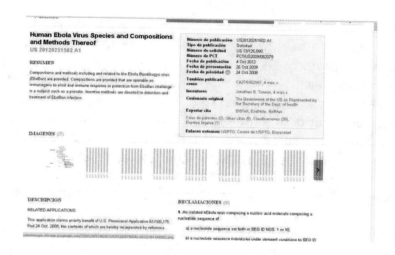

Code: US20120251501502A1

This is what it says on Google:

Compositions and methods comprising and relating to Ebola Bundibugyo virus (EboBun) are provided. Compositions are provided that function as immunogens to elicit an immune response or protection against exposure to EboBun in a subject such as a primate. The inventive methods are directed to the detection and treatment of EboBun infection.

Ebola epidemic of 2014-2016 patented, but patented 2008.

In addition to the above, the Zika virus, which occurred in 2016, is also said to have been patented in no less than 1947.

With Zika, it is not only shocking to know that it is patented, but also that they were selling it for a price of 600 euros. Who? The Rockefellers, another of the most powerful and wealthy families of all mankind.

Although we do not have the patent code for the latter, it is not at all strange to think of it as a very possible possibility.

However, as a reflection, it should be noted and also leave room for doubt. There is the possibility that, although all this is possible, it is actually fake. I know, reading this produces a kind of downer now that your mind was already beginning to be convinced of a new reality or worldview. And that is where I think the "problem" is and where it is not my interest for you to go into. Because I'm not looking to convince you, nor am I suggesting you go down that road.

Moving from one conviction to another will only make you continue to be impregnated with thoughts and more doubts.

This book and this information should be taken with a pinch of salt and more as entertainment than anything else.

Actually, I believe that everything in life has to be taken this way.

What has served me the most is to question absolutely everything and then from there, choose what to believe. But not to choose because of some need, neither you nor I need to believe something. But in this experience it can be useful to us, and that's as far as I go. The "for what" it is useful to you is already your duty. It is true that I may be the one who brings this information to you, but it is also true that this information came to you. Therefore, perhaps more than starting to believe new things, it is time to start unlearning and disbelieving things you used to believe. This is also part of taking off the blindfold.

In the next chapter I will try to bring some calm, peace and love towards all the mental noise that I believe we have been carrying since a couple of years ago when the pandemic and quarantine started. Because yes, it is true that viruses like this had already happened and world catastrophes too, but everything had never been as massive as it is today because of the media and the access to social networks where everything goes viral very fast. So, as much as I will be quite direct in my statements and questions, you will see a reconnection with your inner power. With the creative power that both you and I have.

PLANDEMIC AND OUR MENTAL POWER

As it is the most recent, everything that revolves around theories about COVID, its manipulation andplanning may not be true and we may not be able to conclude anything.

From my perspective, there are some obvious things we can at least comment on:

The use of masks

Okay, let's say it is true that the virus is ultra-contagious and no one is spared, but with the use of masks this would be reduced to almost 0 percent.

Well, it doesn't make sense to me. Even though the use of masks is nothing new, since it is very common in medical centers, now the whole world populationhas the same fear: if I don't use it, I can catch it, so I better use it (even if I don't want to) so I don't catchit. Next thing you know contagion. The mask verse is the same as trying to cover the sun with a finger. Itis the external solution to a fear that is inside.

Social distancing

As the social beings that we are, the fact of relating with others and sharing quality time has very positiveeffects on our organism. There are studies that indicate that by simply giving a hug we already feel more relaxed, gain more confidence and reduce stress.

Why would we stop doing something that seems tohave such good effects on our health?

I was one of those who at first was very sympatheticto all the ideas of distancing. I became obsessed withwashing my hands every time I touched something and even started missing important gatherings of my loved ones to be "careful" not to catch it. Fortunatelyfor me, I moved on and realized that I was just being afraid. It helped me to accept that everything is perfect just the way it is.

Vaccines

Since the problem appeared, this has always been the most desired and expected solution by the majority. Again, an external solution to an internal problem. For me, it was funny to see how they launched a vaccine and a little later they said that

another dose had to be given because the previous one was not so efficient. And then those who ran after the one that seemed to be better. Many times I came to ask myself "seriously no one questions this?"

I could understand that many people may not have had a choice at the time and just went through the process without being a part of it, but others, other people went crazy to get vaccinated.

In the next pages I will talk more in depth about this tool. Of the external solution to an internal problem and our mental power in this process.

The newscasts

If you look closely at the news and even more so at the news that was related to COVID and the pandemic, it was hard not to notice how blatant and exaggerated they were being. All they were doing was saying that people were dying from this virus and that the only thing that was happening was that its spread was increasing. Apparently, for a long time no one else was dying from anything other than COVID. Not only that, but they always justify that they don't tell the whole truth so as "not to cause panic" but with the pandemic it was just the opposite. Strange.

The market and the economy

I remember at the time I was analyzing the financial markets and speculating on the buying and selling of world currencies to make money on the transactions. Although I was not doing well, I was very much into world news as it is the news that most affects the market which is pure collective emotionality. At that time it was part of my daily life to consume news and be aware of what was happening on a financial level in the world.

First hand, I saw for years how manipulated the economy is from the inside. How they continually manipulate the price with fake or delayed news to keep accumulating more money and the big companies keep getting richer and richer.

At that time, there was a lot of talks that the markets could not go on like this as they were at their highest point. That everything that goes up has to come down and that at any moment something was going to happen.

But of course, everything cannot fall just like that. You need some external trigger, like a global catastrophe, to cause a very sharp downward movement. COVID was the perfect tool.

World population

There was a rumor going around that there were already too many of us on Earth and that a kind of purge was necessary. And since the virus mainly affects the elderly, who are considered a burden forthe economy, the business comes out in a big way. Create an ultra-contagious virus and generate fear inall the inhabitants to make it even more efficient. I know this sounds rather cruel, but there is a logic toit. At levels we have no idea, everything is nothing more than pure business.

The war between powers

Shortly before the pandemic broke out, things between the US and China were very tense. It is said that it was planned by the US as a strategic move for economic purposes because China is on its way to becoming the world's greatest power if it is not already. So, by planting this virus there, which we know has the main characteristic of being highly contagious, all products exported by China are going to be considered dangerous so their income would be reduced. (This was more in the beginning, things have changed since then).

Also, others say that China created this virus to make some important economic moves, such as taking over large U.S. companies located in their country that were greatly affected by the emergence of the pandemic.

Undoubtedly, it is a truth that escapes the information we can gather, but there is a cat in the bag. I think it is not about looking for a culprit here, but letting us know how easily we can be manipulated and deceived by generating massive fear in all of us.

The acceleration of digital

It was evident that the avalanche of technology and remote work was coming, but with the quarantine, the speed with which it was introduced was much faster and more abrupt than people expected. Many businesses had to close and many others went bankrupt because they did not go digital, or did not know how to do so.

All this is what is behind a simple virus, but it is backed by fear. And using fear as a weapon of manipulation is nothing new either. The church has been doing it since its beginnings, telling us that there are capital sins that lead you straight to hell. Our mind is unconsciously programmed to avoid pain. This leads us to move more out of fear than out of love. So if all we see outside are contagions and deaths, the seed of fear begins to grow until we reach a point where we no longer doubt that it is true.

I am not saying it is false either. People get infected and people also die, but they are still individual beliefs and as a whole. One with all and all with the whole.

So, you may be wondering, should I completely ignore what is going on in the world? Not necessarily. I believe that within this world there are several worlds. Your mind is one, for example, as well as that of your neighbor, your partner, or your parents. Each person inhabits his reality and it is from there that he creates and contributes to reality as a whole.

That's why you don't need to ignore the rest, it's enough to become aware of yourself.

How would you apply this to the pandemic and everything else that happens?

If we are told to use a mask, use it simply to follow the patterns, but do not believe that the mask is the solution.

If you are told that you have to be vaccinated to continue working or doing X thing, do it if you have no other option, but knowing that the vaccine is not the solution either.

He who knows the fear of people becomes the master of their souls. -Anonymous

I could go on. But then, what is the solution?

Know that there is no problem. That there are simply beliefs. If there is no problem you don't need a solution. So without the need to solve something you don't focus on the problem, you focus on continuing to live your life.

Another way of looking at the rules imposed on us is to do the opposite.

If you are told to isolate yourself, not to hug, fist bump, or wash your hands at every turn, do the opposite.

Bond, hug a lot, hold hands tightly and joyfully and wash your hands if you wish to do so.

What do I mean by that? Don't do anything out of fear. Do what you want to do, but be aware of your emotion behind it.

You can isolate yourself out of love too. You may not hug because you simply don't feel like it or you may fist bump because it's more fun. We can see everything in many ways and none will be right or wrong except the one that resonates with you. With your essence, not with your fear of something happening to you.

All this now allows us to talk about the mental power we all have.

The cure is closer than you think

At any time in your life have you said something like "I'm going to take this because it's good for me" or "I always feel better when I do such and such"?

That was nothing more than yourself conditioning your body to react in a certain way when performing a specific action. Something like the placebo effect: your words and thoughts about something conditioning the effect it may or may not produce.

The placebo effect, although not much talked about, is one of those most incredible mysteries that concerns us all, because we all experience it and use it without even knowing it.

A great book you can read and become much more informed on the subject is "The Placebo is You" by Dr. Joe Dispensa.

To explain the placebo effect in a nutshell, we could say the following:

If you go to the doctor's office and they tell you that X medication works for what is happening to you at that moment, you believe them. How could you doubt it? Well, what if the medicine instead of containing chemical properties were simply sugar wrapped in a pill?

In other words, you are given the same medicine, but in reality, what it contains is something that you consume daily and you do not associate healing properties with it.

Do you think it would produce the same effect as a real drug?

Well, it has been proven that yes. That the simple fact that the patient believes that he is going to be cured with that which he will ingest, he is cured. This is because we gave an order to our mind and it is convinced that it will be so. There is no doubt that what the doctor is giving him is something that will do him good.

And while this may seem like a deception from you to your

mind, the opposite is true. A study was conducted where patients were told that they were going to take sugar pills but that it would have the same positive effect on their health as taking the drug, and the results were positive: patients improved even though they knew they were taking a placebo.

There is a very famous story of Mr. Wright, who was diagnosed with cancer in 1957 and given only a few days to live. Hospitalized in Long Beach, California, with tumors the size of oranges, he learned that a horse serum, Krebiozen, had been discovered that could be effective against cancer. His doctor, Philip West, agreed to administer it to him on a Friday afternoon. The following Monday, outside his "deathbed", the patient joked with the nurses, and days later found that the tumors "had melted like snowballs".

Two months later, Wright read reports calling the serum a quack remedy. He suffered an immediate relapse. The doctor then told Wright, "Don't believe what you read in the papers," and injected him with water, telling him it was a "doubly effective" version of the drug. Once again, the tumor melted. Wright was "the spitting image of health" for two more months until he read a definitive report that the Krebiozen was useless. He died two days later.

Although simple, this story simplifies what I mentioned earlier: your mind has great power to both cures you and make you sick.

The above story makes it very clear how the placebo effect works, both for good and for bad. Both for healing and for curing. Now, let's look at another experiment focused on the other side of the coin, let's talk about the nocebo effect.

Illness is an illusion

Similar, but in reverse. Rather, the nocebo effect describes our ability to believe that something will do us wrong and that this becomes our own premonition.

In 1960, a study looked at subjects with asthma. Researchers gave 40 asthmatic patients inhalers containing nothing but water vapor, but told them they contained allergens or irritants: 9 of them (48 percent) experienced asthmatic symptoms, such as constriction of the airways, and 12 (30 percent) of the group suffered full-blown asthmatic attacks. The researchers later gave them inhalers telling them that they contained a medicine that relieved their symptoms, and their airways reopened for all of them, even though the inhalers contained only water vapor. In both situations, that of provoking asthmatic symptoms and that of eliminating them, the patients responded to the suggestion as the researchers implanted the thought in their minds, obtaining exactly the expected effect.

This begs the question:

How suggestible are we? How much can we modify our state of being? What prophecies are we creating in our minds that can be fulfilled without us realizing it?

I felt it was important to include this information because it is directly related to COVID and the vaccines that revolve around it. Of course the vaccines will do you good if you think so. And of course you will have to give yourself more doses if you are told that one is not enough.

It's not that what's out there is true or not, it's that you are the one who decides if it is.

And of course, the opposite is also possible, that you don't need any vaccines to avoid getting COVID. But if you choose to believe the story that you do need them, well, guess what, you will.

The same thing happens every time you have a headache, fever or get sick. If when something like this happens to you the first thing you do is take a medicine because it is good for you, it will be good for you, but always remember, it is because you think so.

There may also be a belief that you don't need any medication, that the simple act of conscious breathing heals you, or that eating an apple does it. Whatever you do, the point is that you become aware that the external is the external, it is not you, but it directly influences you because it is you who ultimately decides what effect it will have. Whether you are aware of this or not, it is what happens.

At a global level, if we all believe that there is a virus and it is ultra-contagious, we are only being accomplices of our own prophecy. Now, we cannot change the global reality, but we can change our personal reality and from there, contribute to global change.

If our mind is going to be conditioned, whether we want it to or not, let us at least use it to empower ourselves. So that we are not its accomplices, but its owners and creators.

In this chapter I am only reminding you with words and deeds of something that you live and have lived, but that if you do not change you will continue to live.

To end this chapter, I want to show you 3 fascinating stories of the power of the human mind, just as a bonus for you to remember the mental power you have. Even if you are not those people, you are also those people.

Fascinating stories of the powers of the mind

Nina Kulagina

The seminal event on telekinesis is personified by this Russian citizen, who claimed to have psychic powers. For this reason she agreed to conduct her experiments under the supervision of physicists, doctors and journalists.

At one event, Nina not only managed to elevate objects that had been handed to her. She also turned the hands of the clock, managed to paralyze a frog's heart and, through a glance, caused a volunteer's skin to turn reddish.

None of the spectators could refute her work, so much so that the abilities of this psychic were investigated by the Soviet Union during the last twenty years of the 20th century.

Joaquim Argamasilla

In 1923 an extraordinary case was reported in the press. Joaquim Argamasilla, son of the Marquis of Santa Cara, could see the contents of closed boxes, presupposing in him an extraordinary vision. Blindfolded, the boy, then 18 years old, was able to read writings inside closed boxes or to tell the exact time of clocks with the lid closed. Repeated sessions were held at the Marquis' house under the watchful eye of different authorities: notaries, engineers, doctors, physicists, politicians, writers and journalists, which gave the case considerable notoriety.

Ingo Swann

Ingo Swann, who calls himself a consciousness explorer, gained some notoriety among circles interested in the study and testing of such paranormal abilities after he conducted an experiment that involved using his remote viewing to study Jupiter. This happened in 1973, when Swann proposed to Russell Targ and Harold Puthoff to take advantage of the fact that the Voyager probe would visit the planet in 1979, allowing them to verify the information. Among other things, Swann stated that Jupiter had rings around it just like Saturn, which was a matter of scientific discussion at the time and was proven once information was obtained from Voyager.

The experiment led Swann to be contacted by a series of individuals who worked with such secrecy that they never gave him the name of the institution or program to which they belonged, but who proposed to him to use their abilities to explore the Moon. The story is long and complex, but the most important part of the case is that through remote viewing he was able to detect various anomalies on the Moon, including what appeared to be human beings operating on its surface.

THE INCOMPREHENSIBLE AND UNREAL

This chapter is where you can say goodbye to the lid that holds your brain. If you read the book Satseupser, you already know a little about giant anomalies on the sun and ships on the moon, but let me tell you that those chapters don't even come close to comparing to what we will see here.

I believe that everything is a conspiracy, but one thing is the nonsense conspiracies, and quite other those conspiracies that have many points that support them. Once we connect some dots, you will see the immensity of all that is out there. To understand the beastliness of the world of possibilities and to realize how tiny we are, it is necessary to look outside a bit. That's what we'll do here.

The science of extraterrestrial spacecraft and the Aliens' inexhaustible energy source.

No one has shared as much detailed information about extraterrestrial spacecraft and the US government as Bob Lazar, who over the years (since 1989) has shared everything he knows firsthand about the UFO phenomenon in interviews and in hisfamous documentary published on Netflix.

Lazar is a former government physicist who in 1989 made headlines around the world when he first disclosed his study in reverse engineering extraterrestrial spacecraft for the U.S. military. To this day, this gentleman's story is considered to be one of the most shocking in the entire ufological field, so, let's talk a little more in depth about his revelations and who this guy is.

Who is Bob Lazar?

Lazar is a former scientist who worked at a facility designated S4 just south of Groom Lake, part of Area 51. S4 is rumored to be located within the Papoose Range. Lazar says he was hired to work on reverse engineering the propulsion and power sources of ships that he claims were not of this world.

Lazar rose to fame in the late 1980s when he stepped forward, initially using the fake name Dennis, and spoke to local Las Vegas news about thework he says he was doing at S4. This open interviewhe did in 1989, without the cover of a fake name or obscure lights, caught the world's attention. He said he saw flying saucers at S4 and worked on them, trying to break down their propulsion methods.

Is Bob Lazar real?

When Lazar first came forward, they did a thorough background check on him, but could not find any evidence to support his claims that he went to MIT or Caltech (US universities). Lazar claims that there are these discrepancies, possibly created by the government, to discredit him. Instead of focusing on what he says about extraterrestrial technology, people, like these researchers and documentary filmmakers, first spend a lot of time trying to validate basic facts about his past and rarely get past that step.

However, Lazar has his form of proof: he has friends who attest to having picked him up and dropped him off at Caltech. He also points out that he worked for Los Alamos National Laboratory, as evidenced by a telephone directory and a contemporary newspaper article, even though the lab denies that he worked there.

This is more of the same: when important revelations come out, the U.S. secret agency does everything possible to censor it and if necessary even wipe it off the face of the Earth.

In Bob's documentary, he makes special mention of Element 115, one of the most important parts of the whole story that Lazar tells.

In the documentary, he claims that Element 115 not only existed in 1989 when he was in S4 but that a stabilized version is what powers the propulsion of the alien spacecraft. Lazar has hinted in the past that he got something out of S4 before revealing everything in the media, though he has denied it in the decades since and flatly refuses to talk about it in the documentary.

What is surprising about this fact is that element 115 does exist and is known as Moscovium, which was first synthesized in 2003 by a team of Russian and U.S. scientists, many years after Lazar commented on it. As mentioned in the paper, Moscovium is super unstable and a stabilized version would be needed to do what Lazar claims it does.

Area 51, where Lazar claims he worked, was a top-secret place that nobody talked about until then. But when he came out and said that there were flying saucers guarded there, he started to generate a lot of curiosity and intrigue in the whole world about the veracity of his words and what would be inside there.

This is in Lazar's words: "Our job was to see if it was possible to reproduce the technology of those spacecraft with terrestrial materials and systems". During his stay at the base, he had the opportunity to see several UFOs and even penetrated one of them. "It was the same color on the inside as it was on the outside (metallic). There was a central column that went from the floor to the ceiling. It had no angles; it was as if it was made of one piece... The chairs were very small; they seemed to have been made for children. That made me think that it was a ship designed for small extraterrestrial beings, not for human beings.

In addition, Lazar assured in the interview that he saw documents proving the origin of those flying saucers: "There were some documents that indicated that this UFO came from the Zeta Reticuli star system. I have no idea how they knew that.

It wasn't just that it came from the Zeta Reticuli star system, but from a place they called ZR3. It was the third planet in that star system. There was no other information, other than that's supposedly where the ship came from."

Asked what was inside these objects, Lazar said, "I had a very sinister feeling because everything was one color. It was like a dark pewter color. It had no right angles anywhere. It's as if someone took a model and molded it with wax and then heated it for a short time so that everything melted. Everything seemed to be melted. Everything has a radius, a curvature where two objects meet. It's a very strange thing. There was almost nothing, apart from a small folding hatch, that looked recognizable. It was all extraterrestrial."

There were several different UFOs: "One looked like what I called a jello mold. It looked like a classic Jello mold with wavy sides. One was a very flat disk, like a straw hat or something."

But the curious thing is that one of those objects, according to Bob, looked very old: "At least one of them was part of an archaeological dig. So .... was old. I don't know if it was   the   one   I   worked on, but I remember something related to an archaeological dig. That means it was not only old but ancient."

The recent official confirmation that a security identifier that 'scanned' the palm was used in some restricted areas of the Groom Lake facility, as Lazar claimed in the 1980s, accurately confirms his account. In addition, the documentary presented a search of Lazar's workplace by the FBI and other U.S. law enforcement agencies while making the recording as evidence that the scientist was still under close surveillance.

But the most disconcerting part of the report is when Bob Lazar himself, without openly confirming it, hints that he has in his possession the famous element 115, although he inexplicably refuses to talk about it or show it to the public. The documentary insinuates that the recent FBI searches were precisely looking for element 115.

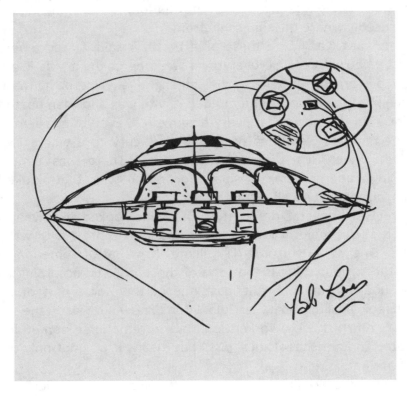

Drawing of the ship Bob worked on in S4.

Bob's story sums up the first statement in the title of this chapter:

The science of extraterrestrial spacecraft: Element 115 in stable form. This provided an energy source with anti-gravitational effects for high energy production.

Now, where did they obtain this element?

Bob says that element 115 was extracted from the sun, since at that time its existence on Earth had not been discovered. Even so, it is still considered an unstable element and therefore there is no possibility of using it as suggested by Lazar, or at least that is what we have been told so far.

To make this a little more visual, in the following pages we will look at some real images taken from observatories that constantly point at the sun and the anomalies that are constantly walking around.

But before we dive into it, let's answer the question that may be on your mind right now...

If antigravity propulsion is real and possible, why don't we use it for space travel?

Well, as we commented, at the moment element 115 is unstable and cannot be used, but a few years ago there was a case where this seemed to be almost a reality.

Anti-gravity technology

One of the pioneering antigravity researchers was Otis T. Carr, one of Nikola Tesla's protégés. Carr, one
of Nikola Tesla's protégés, who built extremely innovative technologies for his time, resembling flying saucers. He even gave public demonstrations sponsored by people who gave millions of dollars for his work.

Otis' goal was to make a flight to the moon on December 7, 1959 with the flying saucer he had built, but as you may suspect, this was not to be.

According to the Center for UFO Studies, Carr's "spacecraft" was powered by an artificial gravitational field called the "Carrotto gravity engine" and used no fuel. Energy was obtained from the Sun through the power of electromagnetism. The technology used is called the "Ultron electric accumulator". But not everything was going to be rosy for Otis, as well as the inventors you will see at the end of this book.

Two weeks after the last test flight, their program was shut down. Federal agents confiscated the equipment and all documentation.

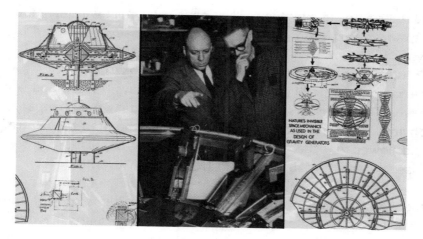

According to them, Carr's project would collapse the U.S. monetary system. He was later charged with fraud and theft of $50,000. Robbed, he was unable to post bail and was sentenced to a 14- year sentence.

After his release from prison, he disappeared from the radar and almost nothing is known about this period of his life. He lived in peace until the end of his days and his antigravity technology was never again released to the public. Antigravity technology was censored and the inventor was silenced.

One thing you dear reader need to know is that what we call the elite have real power over the control of certain things. You see, it is important to understand that there is a world of Secret services. In a recent Michigan State University study, the team discovered that almost 21 trillion dollars were missing, and the U.S. Department of Defense and the

The U.S. Department of Housing and Urban Development did not report any of this.

The money is said to be used for unregistered programs over which Congress has no control. This money is considered the "black budget".

With its help, an invisible civilization is being built with unlimited resources that are far more technologically advanced than the world we know.

Thus, any civilian who   invents a   competitive technology in the black budget world is always tracked and will have difficulty in spreading his invention. What would happen is obvious, since if it reached society it would threaten the control and power that the world elite has over the population. In this case, we also have that of Adam Trombly, the inventor   of   a   power device that   would have   completely   changed the world. In 1980, Trombly and Joseph Kahn came up with the Closed Path Homopolar Generator, a revolutionary invention that could efficiently generate electrical power. Trombly subsequently applied for a patent for his invention and, in June 1982, the International Patent Cooperation Treaty Organization granted the patent with publication number "WO82/02126".

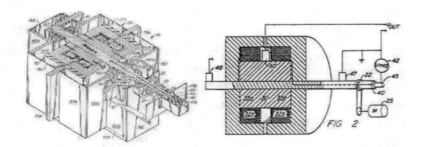

Figure 2: Electrical/Mechanical Schematic View of the Homopolar Generator

Closed Path Homopolar Machine
Inventors: **Adam D. Trombly & Douglas Kahn**
Acme Energy Company: 25 Mitchell Blvd, San Rafael,CA 94903
International Patent Application Number: PCT/US81/01588
International Patent Classification: H02K 31/00, 39/00

Unfortunately, since then, Trombly began to be the victim of a series of attacks, not only against his creation but against his life. Although his invention does not pose a danger to society, on the contrary, it would be a great improvement, it may not go down well with the societies that control energy. In short, Trombly's invention was a generator that, if known worldwide, would represent an impressive improvement in people's lives. This would be a "toothache" problem for the private companies in charge of the electricity supply.

The inventors never thought that this invention could cause them problems, perhaps due to a lack of understanding of reality or a lack of orientation.

What happened was that the private electric utilities felt uncomfortable that their monopoly could be affected and began to attack. With the support of the

U.S. government, these companies began to create problems and attack them so that the two new scientists could not publicly disseminate their generators. Trombly and Kahn suffered a mysterious and unjustified delay in the procedures necessary to legalize their invention, which was essential for it to reach everyone. In addition, the inventor's house was raided, and all the tools used to manufacture the generator were confiscated by the authorities. Everyday around the world inventions and developments are made that can improve the planet, solving the biggest problems (poverty, pollution, energy), however, most of them are all silenced, hidden, and unfortunately their inventors are threatened and even disappeared by a world power ruling interest.

It would be almost impossible for us to know about all the inventions that are made every day in the world and, unfortunately, likely, we will never know about most of the artifacts and innovations that would have a great impact on humanity.

The authorities have never clarified the reason for this violent decision, nor have they returned the stolen artifacts. It was clear that Trombly and Kahn's lives would be in danger if they continued their work. Trombly even claimed that they tried to poison him several times. Trombly never expected to face harassment and death threats for creating a device that brought something good into the world. Today, Adam Trombly remains an internationally renowned scientist, physicist, and developer of Zero Point Energy technology. He has invented numerous New Energy devices capable of extracting energy from the "vacuum", including the "Closed Path Homopolar Machine" and the "Piezoelectric Sound Resonance Generator".

Well, returning to the central theme of antigravity, there is one more case we are going to tell you about.Everything has been hidden in the nature, Viktor Stepanovich Grebennikov was an entomologist scientist, who was mainly concerned with the study of insects, but he was also a painter, naturalist, and lover of the outdoors. He was born in 1927 in Simferopol, a populous city on the Crimean peninsula of what was then the Soviet Union.

Why is this gentleman important? Because in 1988, Grebernnikov was examining insect shells under a microscope when he noticed what he called "an unusually rhythmic, extremely ordered, unparalleled multidimensional solid composition" in the shape of a honeycomb, which looked as if it had been pressed by a complicated automatic machine. As he progressed in the studio something extraordinary happened.

In his words: "I was about to place a second plate with the same unusual cell structure on the bottom, almost on purpose on top of the first one, but then, the first plate came loose from 1000 clamps hanging suspended over the other plate under the microscope for a few seconds. Then, it rotated a few degrees clockwise and swung, and only then fell abruptly onto the desk. When I came to my senses, I tied some panels together with a wire, and it was not easy to do, I only succeeded when I placed them vertically. What I got was a multi-layered titan block, and I placed it on the desk. Even a relatively large object like a thumbtack would not fall on it. Something pushed it up and to the side. When I placed the tack on top of the block, I witnessed incredible and impossible things. The tack would disappear from view for a few moments. It was then that I realized that this was not a lighthouse, but something completely different."

This incredible discovery got Greberdnikov thinking, and science, which suggested that some insects should be too big to fly based on the size of their wings and the speed of their flapping.

Was the structural effect of the cavity caused by this unparalleled honeycomb creating a kind of anti-gravity field that allowed the insects to defy physics and fly?

The insects did not fly, but levitated. Following this line of thinking and the work of past scientists such as Nikola Tesla, Greberdnikov set about trying to create a type of anti-gravitational vehicle. For years, he worked putting heart and soul into the project, until he finally came up with something that possessed seemingly amazing characteristics.

By placing hundreds, if not thousands of titan shells at the bottom of a simple wooden platform, Greberdnikov had invented an anti-gravity vehicle that he claimed could travel up to 1500 kilometers per hour, at a distance of up to 300 meters in height. He operated the device by climbing onto the platform and using two handles attached to the base by a single pole.

Despite the incredible speeds, the driver experienced no effect, no property of inertia or dynamic pressure, almost as if it were installed in a bubble or force field. Moreover, when in flight, the device was invisible from below, appearing only as a sphere of light or a cloud in the sky. Observers noticed that even its shadow was missing when it was in flight, and the clock constantly shifted back and forth. We know from Einstein that time, space and gravity are intertwined. Honored at an invention that could change the world, Grebernnikov believed that so-called real science should investigate his discovery, so he applied for a patent. Surprisingly, his application was flatly denied, while Grebernnikov was rejected and denounced by skeptics and other scientists.

But perhaps the reception of his invention went beyond mere antagonism. In 1932, after his patent application was rejected, Grebernnikov attempted to publish a book detailing his discovery, the principles and measurements of his invention, backed by a number of full-color pictures. It was said that this would include photographs of a demonstration of the machine that Grebernnikov delivered to a museum, however, just prior to the book's publication, publishers, possibly at the behest of the authorities, made dramatic edits to the book removing hundreds of images and all schematic details.

According to a colleague of Grebernnikov's, he said that his friend was part of an underground science, which was persecuted and victimized by the scientific establishment and government entities. Given the money that governments were allegedly spending in pursuit of the secrets that Grebernnikov had apparently discovered, perhaps it is not surprising that his discovery was suppressed. Perhaps Grebernnikov had inadvertently stumbled upon "something" more powerful, and therefore more dangerous than he had imagined. A deep and almost mystical power sought by humans for centuries, one they dreamed of with every UFO sighting or unexplained human artifact.

Think of the great pyramid at Giza, a structure so incredible that generations of deep thinkers have speculated how an ancient society could have created such a thing. It is such an unexplainable mystery that some have suggested that the ancients must have had access to some kind of alien technology. This may not be as far-fetched as it seems.

Recent research shows that the pyramid centralizes and transmits electromagnetic energy to the inner chambers and to the top as in Grebernnikov's honeycomb. Also, in the insect shells of Grebernnikov's flying machine, the scarab beetle was a vitally important symbol in Egyptian mythology, often depicted in art and icons. Strange or not, it appears that the Egyptians may have had access to knowledge since lost to humans, desired by governments and discovered by Grebernnikov centuries later. What exactly he discovered is unknown to this day.

And as Grebernnikov left us in his last words before his death: "There is no mysticism. The thing is simply that we humans still know little about the universe, which, as we see, does not always accept our all-too-human rules, assumptions and orders."

Magnitudes beyond our human understanding a

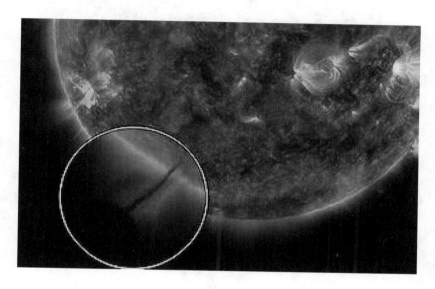

March 2012

March 2016

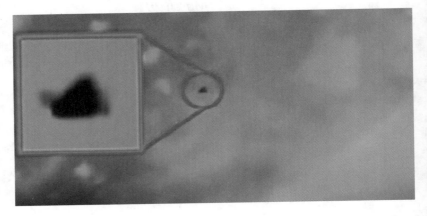

March 2020

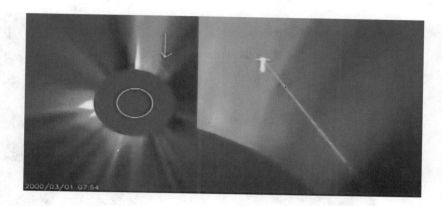

March 2000

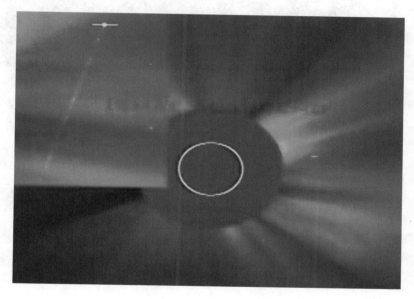

March 2011

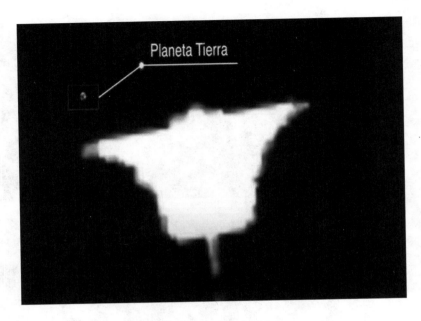

Enlarged image, June 26, 2019

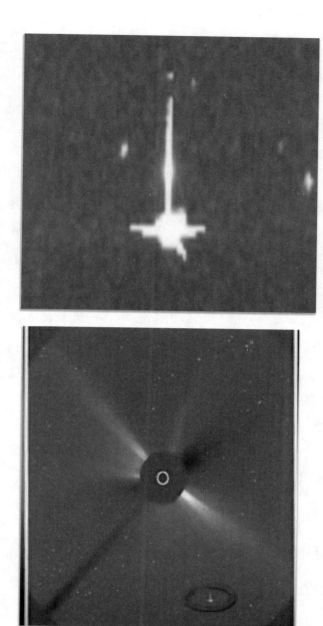

June 15, 2016

Many of these spacecraft or objects that we saw in the previous images are, graphically, gigantic. We are talking about sizes that exceed hundreds of times the size of our planet.

And what do the media and NASA say when something like this circulates? Well, they are simply asteroids, comets, or errors in the recordings. Recordings are made with high-tech cameras to which no one or almost no one in the population has easy access. Particularly, the image that strikes me the most is one of the objects captured on June 26, 2019, since it has a shape very similar to the ships that throughout history have been described. It even looks similar to the one described by Lazar (only, clearly, of a much, much larger size).

This raises the following questions for me:

Are there, at levels we have no idea, giant beings inhabiting even more gigantic ships? Are these objects manned or are they autonomous ships that perform the function of, perhaps, extracting energy from the sun? If they are indeed extraterrestrial spacecraft, what are they doing there, are they our creators or do they know that we do not yet?

Even if I have all these questions, to be honest, I don't think we are even in the same dimension. I don't even think they see us as we see the ants, or maybe that. But this makes one simple thing very clear: they are here, continuously, and closer than we think.

To finish this part, the source of inexhaustible energy of the Aliens may be the sun or any star from which they can extract energy.

And while we're on the subject of giant things, I think it's good to dig a little deeper so that it doesn't get forgotten and your mind has real data.

On YouTube, there is a video entitled "star comparison" which I highly recommend you watch. Below, I will simply leave an

image so that you can read on without going out of context and continue reading, but really, watch the video as soon as you
can:

Comparación de los tamaños de varias estrellas con nuestro Sol

As we can clearly see, even the sun, which is more than 1,294,000 times larger than the Earth, remains very small, almost non-existent even, in front of one of the largest stars observables so far. But it is also not the largest we know of. So, yes, the sun, and of course the Earth, are basically non-existent on a universal scale. Now, imagine you and me there....

Under this comparison, isn't it even logical that there are ships out there, and even beings much larger than us? Up to hundreds of times perhaps.

And yes, we can be suspicious of those objects we see in the sun with very peculiar shapes, but what about these scientific data?

See this image:

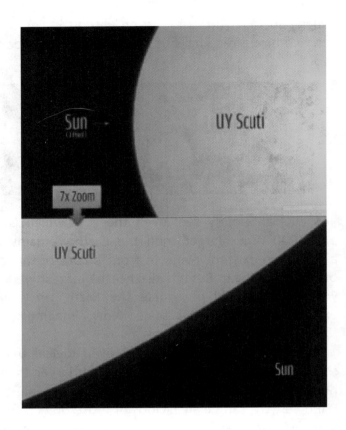

The sun compared to UY Scut

This star is the one that for now is considered the largest in our galaxy, and stay with this last one, onlyin our galaxy.

So, if you still have the lid on your head that holds your brain back, hold it so it doesn't leak out with these other images:

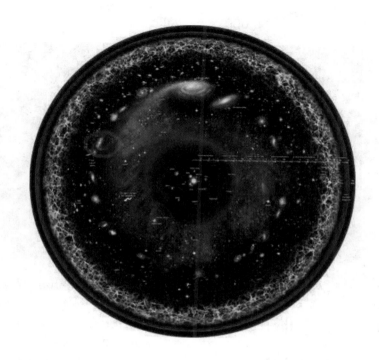

This is the observable universe so far and the red circle is the cluster of galaxies called "Laniakea".

The Laniakea galaxy cluster, which is home to theMilky

Way (red dot) and 100,000 other galaxies.

Our galaxy, where our solar system is located. Which has a mass of 10 to the 12 solar masses.

And you know the rest. From the solar system we go to the planet Earth, then your country, your city, neighborhood, street of that neighborhood, and finally your house. I think we can only marvel at such majesty.

So, before we dive right into our planet Earth, I want us to dive into a possible ancient reality and give more space to the question of whether there will be giant beings out there, because in fact, there is a lot of evidence that says that, yes, there were, but here on Earth.

The ancestors of mankind

Referring to this point, what ends up making a lot of sense is that no one contradicts the evidence that we will see below. On a logical level, knowing the exorbitant dimensionalities of which we are a part, that giants existed here on Earth in the past would not be so far-fetched. But as you know, we will not limit ourselves to simply logical analysis, but we will also look at possible proofs of the truths they have tried to hide from us. The most curious thing is that when one starts to investigate, the only thing that happens is that one discovers the immensity of information that is out there, placed under our noses for us to access the infinite world of possibilities and enjoy the absurdity of human existence.

"And there were giants in the earth in those days, and also afterward, when the sons of God werejoined to the daughters of men and they bore them *sons.* These are the heroes of old, men of renown." -Genesis 6:4

Footprints of giants

Throughout human history, large institutions have largely focused on completely eliminating all evidence of the existence of giant beings. Proof of this was when the world-renowned Smithsonian Institution (scientific research center) sponsored by the U.S. government was forced by the Supreme Court in late 2015 to publicly disclose classified documentation proving that the institute destroyed thousands of skeletons of giant humans in the 1990s.However, in the midst of the trial, a witness appeared in possession of a giant's femur owned by a former Smithsonian Institution official who left a written statement of the reality he witnessed in 1920when the institute had thousands of giant bones stored in warehouses.

Because of this, the institute had no choice but to confirm that they had discarded all archaeological and paleontological evidence for the existence of giants on Earth.

The only detail that the institute did not count on is that the hundreds of giant footprints that have been seen around the Earth cannot be erased and hidden so easily, so the evidence is still very strong.

The question is: what would beings of such dimensions be doing walking barefoot around the Earth? Although the question may seem comical, it seems that we are very far from having any sensible answer to this kind of question. The truth is that we do not have the slightest idea of who they were or what they were doing, the point is that they left more than clear evidence that they were here.

To get an idea, the dimensions of these footprints range from 45 centimeters to 1.30 meters long. Equal to that of humans, with 5 toes, a heel, and a plantar arch.

Hands of giants

A team of archaeologists made a "*macabre*" find around an Ancient Egyptian palace where they found 16 severed hands 3,600 years old in four different pits. All the remains belong to right hands and all are large (between 25 to 31 centimeters long). This indicates that these hands could belong to adult beings of approximately 2.70 to 2.90 meters in height.

Austrian archaeologist Manfred Bietak, who directs excavations in the ancient city of Avaris, explained to the journal Egyptian Archaeology, that the severed hands may be the first evidence to support ancient Egyptian writings about the art of some soldiers cutting off the right hand of their fallen enemies, as it was symbolically believed that cutting them off would diminish enemy forces.

Well, although this finding is still amazing, there is not much evidence or archaeological traces, as well as with feet, but it makes it clear that in ancient times there were beings much larger than the averagehuman being on planet Earth today.

<u>Mega constructions</u>

Another clue that on Earth there were beings with intelligence far superior to that of our times or that they were gigantic beings are the constructions to which to this day no one can give a certain explanation.

Let's start with what may be the most famous and controversial of them all: the pyramids of Giza.

They were built with more than 2.3 million granite blocks, with each block weighing from 2.5 tons to 60tons.

In South America, we have Sacsayhuaman, a megalithic fortress where continuous walls of 9 meters high were erected, made up of blocks of 90, 125 and up to 350 tons each, around 3093 hectares, located in Cuzco, Peru.

And without going too far away, in Peru there is also the city of Ollantaytambo built with monoliths of 12 to 40 tons.

Machu Pichu, a city built with 120- t o n blocks and smaller.

In Asia, the Baalbek platform was built with blocks of rock weighing between 900 and 1100 tons. In the same area, about 7 kilometers from the platform, 3 giant meters of 1000, 1242, and 1650 tons each of equally unknown origins are recognized.

Curiously, in the manuscript of Enoch, chapter 7, it is said that God opened the desert of Dudael, to imprison the fallen angels and the angels that had disturbed humanity. Precisely, this desert is located in Lebanon, where lie the monoliths of 1650 tons of weight.

How were ancient humans able to make such architectural works that are almost impossible to replicate to this day? Did they have extraterrestrial help or were there giant beings capable of moving such tons of weight?

Perhaps both. And while we may not have a clear answer to those questions, we cannot escape the amazing evidence that lies right under our noses at these historic sites.

Before delving further into the obvious and incomprehensible, let's look at a historical document that relates the existence of a woman over 7 meters tall:

In Ecuador, in 1984, the remains of a giant woman were found, which were given to the priest Carlos Vaca, upon his death were analyzed by the Austrian scientist Klaus Dona, who presented the results of this study at the congress in Germany in 2011. The scientist revealed that the remains were those of a giant woman that was about 7.60 meters tall and that inhabited the Llanganates mountain range.

Skeleton in the Jungfrau Park in Switzerland

In addition to these cases, there are many more testimonial documents that relate the existence of beings of lengths between 3 meters to 3.50 meters in height that inhabited different parts of the Earth, but they are nothing compared to the above, which we could say that they are anomalous cases of giantsin an ancient world of giants.

In modern times we no longer see cases of such magnitude,

even if there are humans that measure more than two meters, the world record stands at two and a half meters high, far from the ancient giants that exceeded 3 meters and even more.

All this, related to the colossal dimensions of the universe we inhabit is that it doesn't seem so much like fiction, but begins to make sense. That's why I think we've been kept in the dark and the truth is outthere in bits and pieces. In this book we are putting those parts together so that we can at least see 1 percent of the puzzle.

Anyway, I know that what you have just seen does not entirely convince you since it does not answer questions such as: What is the origin of human beings on Earth? Are we the product of evolution as science says? Are we the product of panspermia? or... Were we deliberately genetically engineered by extraterrestrials of some kind? That's where we will now delve. We will see that what ends up being true is that extraterrestrial, or terrestrial, but much more advanced, beings genetically engineered us.

Dr. Joseph P. Ferrell, author of "The Cosmic War," said, "There was once a very high paleo-ancient civilization, long ago, with science and technology far superior to our own." "That civilization was interplanetary by extension; it existed in our own celestial neighborhoods, fought a war and blew itself up; and as it did so, it realized that it would lose all its high science in the efforts initiated to preserve it." "The rise of the "mystery schools," ancient religions, occult societies, and all such groups since then have been a long-term process of recuperation, and the people involved have done it covertly."

I suggest reader not to overlook the words you have just read, since even the most devout Christian can find a reference in the Holy Bible of the fallen angels, specifically in Genesis chapter 6.

They also came from the heavens and brought with them a very sophisticated technology. The terminology may vary a bit, but the stories that all ancient cultures tell are always the same. So how did humans originate on Earth? Modern "science" would have us believe that humans evolved, but nothing in the ancient remains found has been able to explain how modern man emerged from nothing from cave dwellers to a highly advanced civilization with educational centers and a writing of his own. As it was in the first documented civilization in ancient Mesopotamia.

Modern science can't explain it, but the writings of that civilization most likely can. Researcher Jim Nichols has presented evidence on how our modern world is, in fact, the dark resurrection of a super high-tech civilization that destroyed itself hundreds of thousands of years ago through unchecked weapons science and occult corruption. This theory goes hand in hand with the idea that something beyond man built many of the ancient megalithic structures found around the world, and the secrets behind those structures are held within the global elite and secret societies of Earth.

For what purpose? What do they know? The ancient writings of that first civilization speak of the ancient Anunnaki who were responsible for humanity's "little push" that accelerated the development of intelligent beings on Earth. According to the Ancient Astronaut theory, in the distant past, before the dawn of civilizations, intelligent extraterrestrial beings manipulated human DNA on Earth to create humanity as we know it.

This brings us to the reality that we were genetically engineered in the past, and that it is very likely that we are actually an experiment of a much more advanced civilization.

And although this is a theory at this point, there is one thing that supports it very strongly: the Rh- negative blood type. Humans have four possible general blood types: A, B, AB and O;

this classification is derived, according to scientists, from proteins found on the surface of cells that are designed to fight bacteria and viruses in the human body. The vast majority of humans on this planet have these proteins, which means they are Rh positive. But a smaller group, the Rh-negative, lacks these proteins. So how is this crucial difference scientifically explained, and why does it exist? Over the years, several scientific investigations have tried to find this answer. By all accounts, this would explain why Rh-negative mothers do not tolerate fetuses with Rh-positive blood; thus, this radical intolerance, difficult to explain by most natural laws, could derive from an ancient genetic modification whereby the Rh-positive and Rh-negative groups tend to "repel" each other rather than merge. According to this scientific theory, in the past, extraterrestrial beings came to Earth and created, through "genetic manipulation", the Rh negative with the idea of creating a race of "slaves". The curious thing about this is that the Rh-negative strain is characteristic, for example, of the British royal family, which has generated controversial theories about a possible extraterrestrial lineage. Although this hypothesis has not been confirmed, the disturbing questions it raises are in the air: how would we react to the fact that a small part of the Earth's population has a genetic code altered in the distant past by highly advanced extraterrestrial beings?

Genesis 6:4 "God went in unto the daughters of men, and they brought forth unto them, and they became mighty men of old." From the King James Bible: "women sons - men of Israel, male children ofGod, not sons of man - Ex. 34:23".

Ex. 34:7 says: "The iniquity of the father shall pass to the children unto the fourth generation."

The truth is that there is much evidence that we were visited by beings in the past, not only in biblical accounts, but also in paintings and pictures.

Before we move on to you seeing overwhelming evidence about these visitors depicted in ancient works of art, there is a recent case about a modern-day giant sighting.

This may sound like science fiction to you since perhaps the evidence for giants in antiquity is compelling, but in reality, this would not be possible...or would it?

Giant creature spotted in Canada by a resident that was eventually silenced.

Often the historical facts do not end up convincing us completely because we quickly leave them in oblivion. Well, that is not the case of what we will talk about here, where reality and fiction come together, but also the hidden history and the present converge to give us one of the most incredible mysteries of our epic.

In the year 2022, specifically in the month of April, Andrew Dawson, a tiktoker from Canada, recorded a strange figure at the top of Whistlers Peak Mountains, a 2,470-meter mountain peak located in Jasper National Park in the Trident Range of the Canadian Rockies while on his way to work with his partner.

Andrew managed to capture images of the supposed giant from the moving car and, from then on, became obsessed with the case. He wanted to know what exactly it was that they saw that day and if it was proof of the existence of supernatural creatures. But sadly, that obsession would have been what ended his life. Well, yes, this story does not end as we would like it to.

This is a capture of Andrew's video of the supposed giant he saw in the mountains (note that the image is zoomed in since he filmed it from a distance).

ITS A GIANT

Of course, when you see that image, you might think
it was a pole or something that is fixed there, but in Andrew's
video, you can see it moving.
After the sighting, Andrew devoted much of his time to proving
that he had seen the mysterious snowman. He returned several
times to the scene but found nothing. He tried to climb to the

top of the mountain where he had seen the humanoid, but access was forbidden.

After that, things started to get weirder and weirder. Andrew told his acquaintances that, from his interest in the sighting of the supposed giant, mysterious people began to watch him outside his house and in the places, he used to frequent. He assumed they were CIA agents, who were there because he had seen something he shouldn't have, and not only that: he had also caught it on video.

On April 13, Andrew and his dog Rex got into their truck at 5:32 a.m. to see if they could spot any other strange occurrences on the mountain. That day he again encountered something very curious: an unidentified flying object flying over the mountains where days before he had seen the giant.

Hours later, it passes again along the road towards the mountain, where it showed that they were possibly extracting something with the use of two helicopters. What is interesting about this sequence is that one of the helicopters was holding a tree, a practice they perform after pruning trees in the area, which is not at all strange, but the other helicopter was flying over the mountain in a very curious way that leads us to ask the following question: is it possible that the great attention generated by the first video of the giant on Andrew's mountain caught the attention of government officials who carried out an operation to capture and extract the giant before anyone else saw it? This sounds very similar to the Kandahar giant story of 2002. According to a leaked report by a U.S. official, the U.S. military found a 4-meter-tall giant in a cave in Afghanistan. This giant had red hair, six fingers on each hand, and two rows of teeth. It was aggressive and killed several soldiers before dying. And here is the coincidence with Andrew's case, since, immediately after his death, a large military helicopter was sent to the site to pick up the giant's body and transport it to a secret military facility.

On April 14, Andrew returned to the same mountain pass, where days before he had been stopped by a possible CIA agent, to try his luck this time. There he shows a car blocking the road and a guy outside the car stopping Andrew, who told him that the road was closed and that he should turn around.

"I don't understand why it's closed, whether it's a public parking lot or public road, I don't know," the man commented after walking away from the past.

Three days later, Andrew uploads a new video to his TikTok account, where he shows that the same car that was slowing down the mountain days before, was outside his house. He decides to face them by going outside his house and calling out to them, but the car accelerates and gets lost on the road.

After several days without any update, on May 9 he uploaded on his TikTok account a new video updating about the whole thing, saying that he has not died and had not disappeared either. He then stated that the previously posted videos were fake and were only for entertainment, for which he apologized.

What made the video strange was Andrew's position in front of the camera, with his hands in his pockets and looking to his left at one point. Many suspected that Andrew had been forced to deny everything.

In his next video posted on May 16, Andrew titled it "I'm scared", accompanied by the following description: "A lot of things have happened, and I can't be forced to keep quiet". In the recording, Andrew is seen nervously walking inside his home and looking worried. "You may not see my post anymore, my videos are not fake," Andrew said while recording the video. The next day, Andrew publishes his last video related to the subject, where he shows an alleged military vehicle on top of the mountain, in the same area as the possible giant's appearance. "This wasn't there yesterday," were Andrew's last words in the video.

Andrew was very prolific on TikTok and had talked openly about what he saw in the snow. But Andrew didn't live long enough to find out more. Days after his last post, he passed away under mysterious circumstances. His obituary in the Campbell River Mirror says Andrew Ryan Watchorn Dawson was born Nov. 4, 1987, and died July 1, 2022. "Beloved husband, father, uncle, brother, and son." It could have been a coincidence, but many of his followers believe it had to do with him "knowing too much." He had in his possession sensitive information that could prove the existence of things the government seeks to keep secret.

We know that for you to hear this is not very new, since we have already mentioned several inventors who were silenced as well, but it is pertinent to remember at this point in the book that the truth is there, but they are wanting to hide it at all costs.

You may or may not have heard of this case, but we decided to include it in this book because it merges two very important things:

1.   The existence of giants even today
2.   The government's strong censorship of these issues

Well, we know that this story has a lot more power when you watch the videos and listen to what Andrew says, how he says it, and what he feels. For this reason, we are not going to leave you with a simple image of low quality where you see a possible giant backed by a story of a boy from Tiktok, so, if you want to see the saga of videos of what Andrew filmed and so you can corroborate with your own eyes what you have read here, write us to our email conscienciadisruptiva23@gmail.com telling us that you read the story but want to see all the videos in Spanish, because yes, the originals of Andrew are in English but we have subtitled them so you can understand perfectly what he says.

Now, to add more mystery to the historical facts, let us remember that our ancestors already believed in angels, extraterrestrial ships, and luminous spheres, so much so that they left evidence of them everywhere. This we will see below.

UFOs everywhere

Many people believe that this UFO phenomenon is something new. Something that we are just now beginning to see something about. But that is far from reality. For centuries, ancient cultures have already alluded to ships and beings that do not seem to be from Earth. All over the world, such manifestations have been seen in caves, pictures and paintings. We will see that below. I did not limit myself at all when placing here all those images that I considered relevant to the subject because I do not want anything to be left out, or at least as little as possible. I should point out that in some of them there is a more mythological explanation, so let's start with the most famous, the wondjina (or wandjina), of the Australian Aborigines, a hunting society of whom there is evidence since 174,000 BC.

Paintings on the Wandjina in Australia
Located in different parts of the oceanic country, these anthropomorphic drawings represent the spirits of rain and clouds, and were the creators of life on earth. In addition, they had special powers such as causing floods and intense lightning.

Another case of anthropomorphic beings that arouse curiosity was discovered in India, in the tribal region of Bastar, Chhattisgarh.

And what can this tell us? That humans of ancient times saw, or imagined, beings coming from another part of the cosmos.

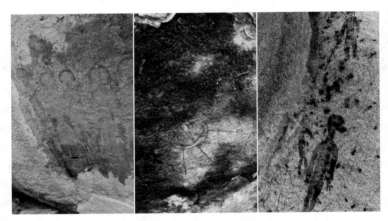

Some of the drawings in the caves of Chhattisgarh (The Indian Times).

As you can see, these figures are dated 10,000 years old, and among them there are shapes that refer to the UFO phenomenon and strangebeings.

Also in India, another finding generated controversy due to its incomprehensibility. In the Narmada valley, where the oldest human skull in that country was found, a group of researchers (R.P. Pandey, Wasim Khan and K.W.Shah) discovered in a shelter called *Rajatole* a painting that seems to represent a strange visitor next to a ship and even a wormhole, together with a large number of small stone tools from the Mesolithic periodscattered on the floor.

The figures of the Rajatole shelter in the Narmada Valley
In Italy, for instance, there is the UNESCO- protected Val Camonica valley, which has about 200,000 petroglyphs dating from the Neolithic to the Iron Age, making it the largest collection of rock art in Europe and the world.

Among them are some that have been taken by subscribers to the ancient astronaut theory as expressions of beings from other planets - because of the helmet-like shape seen on their heads, although for archaeologists they are simply an expression of a ritual.

Petroglyphs in Val Camonica

In the American continent, from the USA to Argentina (caves in Mendoza and La Rioja), there are also remarkable examples of figures that are puzzling. Just to name a few cases, in Utah, in Barrier Canyon, within the Cannyonlands National Park, there is a series of stone drawings with anthropomorphic characterizations.

In Bolivia, there is the mysterious Fort of Samaipata at 1950 meters above sea level (a UNESCO World Heritage Site since 1998), apparently built as a ceremonial center between the 14th and 16th centuries, which houses a petroglyph with a definite UFO shape.

Above: a petroglyph from Utah. Below: anthropomorphic beings found in La Rioja, Argentina, and next to them the 'flying saucer' of the Fort of Samaipata.

Also in Puebla, Mexico, a group of treasurehunters found, in 2017, a set of carved jade stones that leave little room for double interpretations: Mayas are seen exchanging offerings of large, elongated-headed beings.

One of the carved jade stones found in caves in Puebla.

And well, when we say art we are not only talking about pictures and paintings, also in books and texts we can find allusions to strange beings and objects that came to Earth. The first book that is known with some kind of figure discordant with its time is the *Prodigiorum liber*, from the fourth century, where we read: "In Aenariae, while Livius Troso was promulgating the laws at the beginning of the Italian war, at dawn, there came a tremendous noise in the sky, and a globe of fire appeared in flames in the north. In the territory of Spoletum, a globe of fire, golden in color, fell to earth spinning. It then seemed to increase in size, rose from the earth and ascended into the sky, where it obscured the sun with its brightness. it turned towards the eastern quadrant of the sky."

This is how Julius Obsequens described the event that occurred around 91 BC.

Book of Prodigies

In the Archbasilica of St. John Lateran, inside the Vatican State, there is a reliquary box that has aroused various speculations over the years, especially because of one of the drawings inside.

The reliquary, according to the Holy See of Roman Catholicism, is one of the first testimonies of the custom of taking objects as souvenirs of the trip to the Holy Land and its style and iconography suggest it is of Palestinian origin, with Syrian influences.

Inside of the reliquary

Dating from the 6th or 7th century, this treasure has images painted on the inside of the lid that can be read in a precise ascensional manner (from left to right and from bottom to top), to delineate the "Christmas" cycle (with the Nativity and the Baptism in the Jordan), followed by another equally brief "Easter" cycle (with the Three Marys at the tomb and the Ascension), divided by the central scene of the Crucifixion.

Among these images there is one that represents Mary at the tomb of Jesus, while behind it rises a strange object, with a dome with different entrances or windows from where a beam of light comes out.

From "The Book of Good Customs".
One of the interior illustrations of the 1338 text, which is in the Musée Comte de Chantilly, France, shows a large sphere floating in the sky, which to some may be an astronomical representation or a ship of some strange kind.

At that time, *Annales Laurissenses Maiores*, a book dating from the 12th century A.D., but telling stories from the 6th century, was also produced. There, it is illustrated with an image in which two objects appear with a modern spacecraft aesthetic. They even seem to move from a combustion system, although the official reading of the illustration dictates that they would be comets or meteorites.

"...and on the same day, as they prepared for another assault against the Christians living in the castle, the Glory of God was manifested above the church of the fortress. Those who were watching in the square outside - many of them are still alive today - said they saw something that looked like two large flaming shields of a reddish color moving around the church," explains the work by unknown authors.

From "Annales Laurissenses Maiores".

Returning to some of the most controversial works, we have the *Madonna of San Giovannino*, painted during the Renaissance, which today can be seen in the Palazzo Vecchio, Florence. It is unknown who was the author of this oil on canvas, although specialists have two candidates: Sebastiano Mainardi or Jacopo del Sellaio.

The presentation of Mary, with her son and a small St. John has been a very popular theme in this era of art. Boticelli, Leonardo, Raphael and Michelangelo made their versions, although this one has a peculiarity: to the right of Mary's head there is a strange flying object in the background.

"The Madonna of San Giovannino."
The artist also did not want the figure to go unnoticed, and for that reason he also painted a person, possibly a shepherd, who observes the artifact with great attention together with his pet.

This is not the only religious painting where something strange is perched in the firmament. Another notable example is the *Annunciation with Saint Emigdio* (1486), by the Italian artist Carlo Crivelli.

The piece was made to commemorate the announcement of the archangel Gabriel to the Virgin Mary, although the interpretation of the figure from which the beam of light is emitted depends on who you ask.

The "Annunciation with St. Emigdio" and "The Baptism of Christ".

Another work with a similar polemic is *The Baptism of Christ* (1710), by the Dutchman Aert De Gelder, Rembrandt's pupil, inspired by the biblical passage of Matthew 3:16, from the New Testament: "The heavens were opened, and the Spirit descended upon him like a dove".

In the work, a circle opens in the sky and gives off light beams towards the center of the scene, while a tiny bird seems to descend.

But not all the pieces have such a simple explanation. For example, *The Triumph of Summer* is a tapestry dated 1538, which was made in Bruges, Belgium, depicting the rise of a ruler to power. It is now in the Bavarian National Museum in Germany.

The triumph of summer

This decorative piece has on the left and on the right several objects in the shape of a hat or a classic flying ship: a disk with a crew dome.

The Life of the Virgin found in the basilica of Notre-Dame de Beaune, in Burgundy, France, which was erected in the 13th century and has Gothic and Renaissance elements. But it is not its architecture that most attracts the attention of religious tourists and the curious in general, but it houses a beautiful tapestry of the fifteenth century.

"The Life of the Virgin", in the Basilica of Notre-Dame de Beaune

The tapestries were a fashion that originated around the 14th century and lasted until around 1530, when the Council of Trent asked to remove everything that did not allow the faithful to follow the service. In front of them, which were intended to tell some story from the bible -of the virgin and Jesus in general- the choirs were usually placed. In this tapestry appear figures very similar to those of *El triunfo del Verano*.

But these are not the oldest depictions of a flying saucer-like figure. In a 10th century piece from the *Prajnaparamita Sutra* (The Perfection of Wisdom Sutras), a collection of about 40 stories of Indian origin between about 100 BC and 600 AD, a

number of mysterious ship- shaped objects also emerge.

In *Glorification of the Eucharist* (1600) by the Italian Ventura Salimbeni, the figure of the orb (sphere of luminous light) appears once again. This altarpiece gained notoriety in ufology because the object between Jesus and God has a shape very similar to the famous Sputnik, the Russian satellite that started the space race with the USA in 1957.

"Glorification of the Eucharist" and an image of Sputnik.

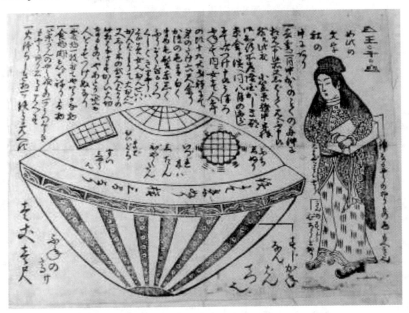

Illustration of "Utsuro-bune", by Nagahashi Matajirou in 'Ume-no-chiri' (1844).

In Japan there are three texts describing experiences with the *Utsuro-bune* (Japanese for hollow boat): *Toen shōsetsu* (1825), *Hyōryū kishū* (1835) and *Ume-no-chiri* (1844). They recount the landing of a mysterious object found drifting off the coast of Hitachi province of eastern Japan in 1803.

The illustration portrays the characteristics of the object the sailors found floating in the ocean. From the "hollow boat" came down a woman, who, not speaking Japanese, returned to her ship and was lost at sea. For Japanese folklorists it is just a story, for ufologists, irrefutable evidence.

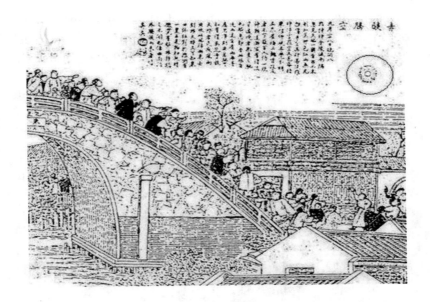

"Red flames in the sky", by Wu Youru.

A few decades later, in 1892, Wu Youru, one of the first Chinese cartoonists, presented his *Red Flames in the Sky*, in which he recorded a strange event that happened on the ZhuqueBridge next to the Fuzi Temple in Nanjing.

Also in Asia, there is a Tibetan manuscript, dated in the 10th century. In a passage of the *Prajnaparamita Sutra* (The Perfection of Wisdom Sutras), the Vimanas, a flying vehicle of Hindu origin, is depicted. The text assures that it flew with "the speed of the wind" and gave birth to a "melodious sound".

Prajnaparamita Sutra

This is just one representation of these vehicles, which, belonging to the religious order, appear in many works, such as *The Flower Ship* (1916), an illustration by Bala Sahib for the book *Chitra Ramaiana*.

"The Flower Ship" (1916), an illustration by BalaSahib.

Well, all this points to the fact that flying objects and extraterrestrial beings are nothing that has not been seen before. And to focus a little more on the present day, not only on the sun or in ancient paintings objects are seen, but also on the moon.

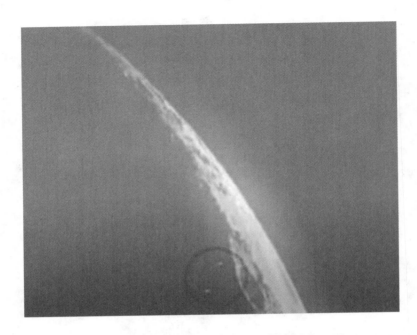

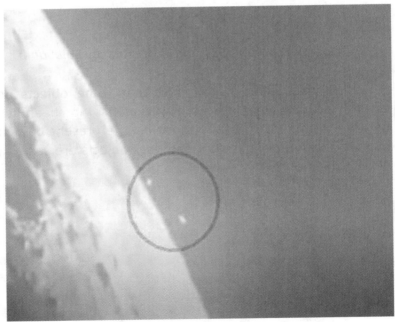

These two images are from April 4, 2020, andalthough the quality is not the best, we can see two spheres circling the lunar surface, which nobody knows what they are.

Now, there is something much more shocking than these images. There was an unidentified object that was hovering above us for a while and was first seen on October 19, 2017.

Oumuamua: the interstellar visitor

This strange object first appeared in October 2017 and was so named by astronomers at the University of Hawaii's Pan STARRS continuous sounding system Pan STARRS (Oumauamua means "messenger from far away that arrives first, in Hawaiian).

The telescopes were able to follow its trajectory for about three days until they lost sight of it. It is said that it was not a normal object, since it was 400 meters long and its width was ten times smaller. It also had a reddish surface.

At first, it was believed that Oumuamua could be one of two

things: either a comet or an asteroid. But very soon the option appeared that in reality, its origin could be artificial.

By saying that it may be artificial, we mean that it may be a fully operational probe intentionally sent to the vicinity of Earth by some extraterrestrial civilization.

In addition to this possible theory, its unusual behavior, and characteristics, as well as the fact that it is the first object discovered in the Solar System that originated outside the Solar System.

In addition, Oumuamua is composed mostly of nitrogen, which is a rare element that has only been found on Pluto and is only 0.5% of the total mass of the dwarf planet. Not only that, but scientists believe that there is not enough nitrogen in the universe to generate an object of the dimensions of our interstellar messenger.

So, could Oumuamua be the irrefutable proof that life exists on other planets?

Maybe yes and maybe no, but that brings us that much closer to a world largely unknown to all humans, it does.

As Sherlock Holmes said, "When you eliminate all logical solutions to a problem, the illogical, though impossible, is invariably true."

Testimonials from astronauts, former CIA agents and airline pilots on their sightings

Helen Sharman

In 1991, Helen Sharman spent eight days in space, where she joined the Soviet mission to the Mir space station. She was 27 years old at the time and has given very strong statements saying that extraterrestrials exist and that with so many billions of stars in the universe there must be all kinds of different forms of life.

Edgar Mitchell

He was the pilot of the Apollo 14 moon mission. Mitchell claims that he has been aware of many UFO visits to Earth during his career, but all have been covert. He describes the aliens as small beings "that looked at us strangely".

Deke Slayton

Deke participated in the Mercury project, a program whose purpose was to take man to the Moon. This astronaut was on several NASA flight team missions; however, while performing his job, he reportedly saw an extremely strange craft and said: "It looked like a saucer at a 45-degree angle, after a while it started up and took off, and I couldn't see it anymore".

Brian O'Learly

NASA, in its early years, had planned to carry out a project to travel to Mars. O'Learly was part of it, however, the plan was cancelled. Nevertheless, Brian became an academic at Cornell University alongside Carl Sagan. After his retirement, the former astronaut assured about the existence of extraterrestrials on Earth; he also maintained that these beings would contribute to the technological advancement of our planet.

O'Learly said the following:

"Other civilizations have been monitoring us for a long time. Their appearance is strange from a Western point of view."

Gordon Cooper

He accumulated no less than 222 hours in space. He was one of the astronauts in NASA's Mercury Program. In 1963, he piloted the Faith 7 spacecraft for more than 34 hours. He also commanded the Gemini 5 mission. He retired from NASA in 1970. In 1985, he testified before the United Nations that the United States was detecting unknown objects on its radars on a daily basis and that the U.S. government was forcing astronauts and scientists to keep all this secret.

So stated Gordon Cooper:

"I believe that those extraterrestrial craft and their crews visiting Earth from other planets are obviously more technologically advanced than we are. I think we need a very high-level coordinated program to collect and scientifically analyze the planet's data on the various types of encounters in order to determine how best to act amicably with our visitors. It would first be necessary to show them that we learned to solve our problems peacefully and not by war, before being accepted as a full member of the universal team. I am sure that being admitted would offer our world fantastic possibilities for progress in all areas. For years, I have lived with a secret, the secret imposed on all specialists and astronauts. Now I can reveal that every day, in the United States, our radars detect objects of unknown shape and nature. There are thousands of eyewitness reports and documents to prove it, but nobody wants to publish them. Why? The authorities fear that people imagine some kind of horrible invaders. So the slogan remains: we must avoid panic at all costs."

Heidemarie Stefanyshyn-Piper

One of the most extraordinary and clear UFO cases happened in the STS-115 mission of the Shuttle Atlantis, in 2006. Among the crew members who saw strange devices near the Shuttle was Heidemarie Stefanyshyn-Piper; the objects were captured on video: five spheres and a kind of cylinder. It was obvious that something had "intercepted" the approach of Atlantis to Earth, but... who better than the astronauts to tell exactly what they saw? That role fell to Heidemarie Stefanyshyn-Piper, but her live appearance ended dramatically when she fainted while trying to explain what they had seen.

"It was something that had never been seen before," the female astronaut said at that NASApress conference.

In total there were two continuous fainting spells. She would try to speak, but would immediately stagger and lose consciousness. What was the subsequent official explanation? Space junk, ice crystals, etc.

These accounts from former astronauts andpilots of the U.S. armed forces leave us with clear evidence that there is information that they do not want to reveal to us for the simple reason of wanting to "protect us" and that over the years thousands of sightings have happened, and continue to happen.

More than believing or not believing these testimonies, what is behind them is something simple: there are objects out there and although we don't know what they are, they don't want to tell us what they do know.

Shocking photographs of underwater UFOs

What we will see in the following pages are photographs taken in March 1971 from a U.S. Navy submarine between Iceland and Jan Mayen Island in the Atlantic Ocean.

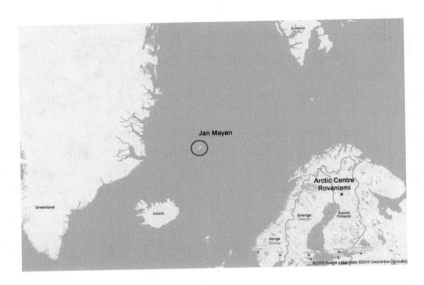

Location of the Island

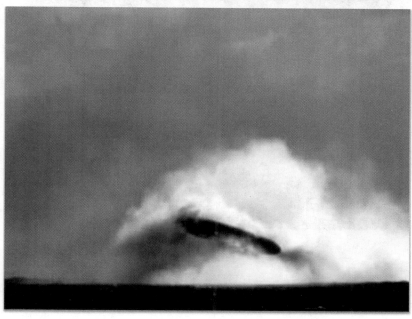

In all this journey, of the incomprehensible and unreal, I think we can deduce the following: we have no idea of anything, at least I don't think we do, but there is something we cannot escape from the imminent evidence of flying objects on Earth, of giant objects, of objects visiting us, of giant beings that inhabited Earth and that the elite or whatever we want to call it has hidden much of all the information from us. I think it may all be incomprehensible to our human mind, but something within us resonates with this. I think one recognizes the truth when one feels it. It is also unreal, because our senses, our mind, are not adapted to believe in such dimensions, such, that would nullify its existence and in turn, make it part of the whole. Therefore, in the next and almost last chapter, we will talk about this. The nothing and the everything...

NOTHINGNESS AND EVERYTHING

Two sides of the same coin. Everything and nothingness do not exist and exist at the same time.

In this chapter, we are going to go beyond the limits of our mind, because here you don't need it. You don't need to try to understand anything, just let yourself be soaked by the abundance of incomprehension, letting it take you to universal levels where everything makes sense, and nothing makes sense, at the same time.

The same point that composes everything composes nothingness, so talking about them plunges you, without asking, into the point of equilibrium. Let me go deeper into this: when you begin to conceive of spacetime as "all there is," what is that all? Where is it?

According to research, "the whole" contains nothing but space. And how do this manifest itself in the objects we see and the reality we conceive? Easy, through our 3D perception of the world as a physical construction of objects and shapes.

The curious thing is that we have convinced ourselves for millennia of this truth. The truth is that what we perceive is the only thing there is or the only real thing.

Through our spectrum of vision, we are not able to perceive more than a very small part of all the electromagnetic waves that exist in the cosmos. According to Dr. Karan Raj, the human eye is only capable of perceiving 0.0035% of reality.

"What is essential is invisible to the eye."
The Little Prince

This confirms something very obvious: our reality is limited, or else limitedly false.

And not because it is not real at a total level, but because we believe it is real.

The point of understanding that everything and nothing are the same leads us to the point that contains them, to nothing and everything unified in something.

What is this something? In the followingchapters we will see different points that couldhelp us to answer this question.

We will talk about totality and nothingness itself. First, under more spiritual points, then we will approach some of the theories created by people who tried to put down in more technicalwords these concepts.

The music of the stars

To understand one of the greatest secrets of humanity and to know that "everything and nothing" together, talking about acoustic levitation can bring us closer to understanding how this universe works.

Acoustic levitation is the experience of lifting in space (something or someone) without the intervention of known physical agents. We can understand levitation as floating in the air without anything to hold the object or person. And when we speak of acoustic levitation, we refer to the fact that the reason why the object or person floats is because of some sound or sound frequency that causes it to levitate.

The first thing to think about is, how is this possible.

To put ourselves a little more in context, the universe as we know it is composed of energetic frequencies, i.e. everything is composed of energy vibrating in the whole, or in nothingness itself.

Under logical deduction, you and I are also energy, just like a rock, a tree, your computer, and everything around you.

Then, by accessing certain vibrational waves, we could make objects levitate, or even make ourselves levitate.

There are many legends about people with the ability to levitate by entering into deep states of meditation where, according to what they said, they accessed altered states of consciousness and stopped contemplating themselves as a physical body, and in that world, they were able to do anything, one of them, levitate.

Of these stories, as much as we can find them on the web and they seem true, many theories with great validity disprove their actions and end up proving that they were simply tricks they used to deceive people, so I did not consider it relevant to mention any specific one.

Even so, there is a very impressive case of a sculptor who built a park of rock gates, alone, without the help of any (known) instruments or people.

Edward Leedskalnin, who was born in 1877 in Latvia, became one of the most impressive acoustic levitation enigmas of all.

At the age of 20, he settled in Florida, USA, where he began the construction of his life: his rock gate park, a sprawling stone city made of more than 1,000 tons of coral rock, stones weighing up to 35 tons each.

People who knew about this sculptor began to wonder how a man with tuberculosis could have maneuvered, cut, and shaped all that rock into place by himself.

In 1986, long after his death, the gate of the park, then called Coral Castle, broke and it took 6 men with a 45-ton crane to fix it.

Leedskalnin never revealed his secrets, only saying that he "knew how to tune in to the music of the stars."

In the words of the sculptor:

"I have discovered the secrets of the pyramids and have found out how the Egyptians and the ancient builders of Peru, Yucatan, and Asia, with only primitive tools raised and placed stone blocks weighing many tons."

In addition, his neighbors claimed to have heard him singing to their coral. Also, a group of teenagers swore they had seen him floating blocks of coral-like hydrogen balloons. Simple.

Most tellingly, a large stockpile of radio equipment was found in the depths of the castle, as well as a soundproofed and hermetically sealed room that could have been used for sound experiments.

Another striking story is that of a Swede known as Dr. Jarl, who, in the 1930s, came to Tibet to a place where few people had been before. Jarl was invited there by a friend he had in Tibet to treat a prominent lama who had fallen ill.

An account of Jarl's trip was published in a German magazine, detailing his time in Tibet and a most extraordinary story:

According to the Doctor, one day he was taken to a meadow surrounded by high cliffs. In one of these cliffs, about 250 meters off the ground, was a cave and the beginnings of what appeared to be a stone wall being built by the locals. Jarl wondered how it was possible to do such a thing since there was no way to the ledge except perhaps by hanging a rope.

He noticed with curiosity that in the barren meadow was a huge slab of polished rock with a bowl shape carved in the middle.

At one point, a group of monks carrying massive instruments appreciated.

These monks brought with them huge iron drums and 3-meter-long horns. The monks used an ox to drag a substantial rock over the smooth slab of rock in the meadow. They then placed their instruments around it and began to play by beating the iron drums with leather mallets and blowing their horns. What happened next shocked Jarl: when the stone was in place, the monk behind the small drum gave a signal to begin the concert. The little drum had a very high-pitched sound and could be heard even with the other instruments making a terrible din. All the monks were chanting and intoning a prayer, slowly increasing the tempo of this incredible noise. For the first 4 minutes nothing happened, then, as the speed of the drums and the noise increased, the big block of stone began to sway and sway, and suddenly took off into the air with increasing speed in the direction of the platform in front of the hole in the cave, 250 meters high.

After 3 minutes of ascent, he landed on the platform. Amazed, Jarl watched the modes repeat this process over and over again, moving 5 to 6 rocks every hour as the rock wall slowly grew. He couldn't believe his eyes, assuming he might have been hypnotized or drugged. So he set up a camera to record the process. When he saw what he recorded, he saw exactly what he had seen: rock by rock levitating as if by magic. The curious thing is that when Jarl returned to Europe, the scientific society that had sponsored his trip confiscated his videos and they subsequently disappeared.

So, was Jarl hypnotized or did these monks have secret knowledge that could levitate rocks in the air? Was this a similar experience to what the sculptor in the previous story was done with rocks to build his park?

Today we know that acoustic levitation is nothing that cannot be done, therefore, these stories do not necessarily have to be mere legends or myths.

In acoustic levitation, the sound is used to counteract the force of gravity, simply because when sound waves bounce off a surface, the interaction between the compressions and refractions created causes interference.

Occasionally, reflections and interference combine to create what is called a standing wave. These are sound waves that appear to vibrate rather than travel from one place to another.

Fundamentally, when the orientation of the standing wave is parallel to the force of gravity, the effect is levitation. These standing waves are created using an acoustic levitator (a device composed of a transducer, a vibrating surface that creates sound, and a reflector).

The monks' transducers were the drums and horns, the reflectors the smooth slab of rock with its concave surface.

Something very important is also the distance from what we call the transducer to the object to be moved, it must be very precise.

But we don't need to go into so many details, let's just stay with what is behind all this: an invisible field that moves by vibration waves where everything is connected with everything, through certain sounds/frequencies.

"The secret lies in the geometric placement of the musical instruments about the stones to be levitated and the harmonic tuning of the drums and trumpets."-Bruce Cathie

So, if there is a field that we are all part of, that is there all the time with us and that we can access whenever we want, can we claim that we have an infinite mind? I mean, what is the limit of our possibilities in this physical experience we are living here on Earth? Are we humans simply a physical body,

meant to eat, sleep andreproduce, or do we also have access to all this
Ancestral knowledge to create, literally,whatever we want?

The infinite mind

The mind, our infinite mind. What we saw about acoustic levitation does nothing more than explain what both you and I experience all the time: the energetic vibration and inexplicable connectivity of all "things". The wonderful thing about this is that, as parts of a whole, our mind becomes infinite, infinite in possibilities of events. "Everything" is events or probabilities of events, however, we look at it.

Understanding that we possess an infinite mind opens up a world of endless ways of seeing what happens or creating what happens.

From a level of separation, things just happen. From a level of unity/wholeness, everything you are happening, because there is no real separation. Separation of events is only a mental creation.

Seeing ourselves as infinite beings with an infinite mind allows us to detach ourselves from our egoic limits governed by a form where there is no contemplation that anything can happen because it is already happening.

Let's bring this down to earth a little bit: you are reading a book to know the only truth was one of the many possibilities that there were for you to believe that such a book existed. From my perspective, I created the book, but the truth is that, for you to read it, you must have been able to create that event, because I do not know you, nor did I know that a book with this title would be read.

To choose the name, I chose from the infinite number of possible options, all possible and all existing in the universe of infinite possibilities.

Where I am going with this is that we are all creating, all the time, as everything creates itself. It is nothingness itself merging into everything. Or is everything being nothingness itself?

This is what scientists have called wave or particle behavior in energy. Dual behavior depends on who is looking at it.

Therefore, this book may contain all the truth and be very revealing for you, but another may hate it and find it completely useless.

From my point of view, this book contains the whole truth, because you already are the whole truth. In minds with lacking beliefs, lacking "of", this book will be lacking.

The marvelous thing about the Whole is that each part represents the totality. Therefore, to understand the truth it is not necessary to know everything, it is enough to know nothing. Or, to not believe that we need to know something, thus allowing us to contemplate ourselves as part of the truth and then live it.

Shades of reality

As we mentioned at the beginning of this chapter, we know that our ability to see at the spectral level is less than 0.1 percent. Doesn't this only underscore everything we have discussed in this book? Remember, possibilities. We are very limited in the level of focus when it comes to assimilating the totality of the cosmos. In reality, all that the universe contains goes far beyond all our senses. It is difficult to dimension the enormous amount of things that we are not able to perceive.

To go deeper into this, we can draw on some paragraphs from Jacob Grinberg's book entitled The Synergistic Theory, Chapter V, which he entitles The Directionality Factor:

We could see a landscape, decode the image of the craters of the moon or perceive a distant galaxy because each point of the latice contains the information of them. The fact that the resulting image is that of the landscape or object and not another means that we have focused attention, this phenomenon is called the directionality factor. Don Juan Matus, the shaman from Sonora, calls it Anchor Point. The lattice and the existence of the synergic bands explain this human condition of being an instrument of reception of a more expanded consciousness.

All these relativistic effects seem strange because with our senses we do not experience four-dimensional space-time but can only observe its "three-dimensional reflections". These effects will seem absurd if we do not realize that they are only the three-dimensional projections of phenomena that take place in four dimensions, just as shadows are projections of three-dimensional objects.

Exploring the field of philosophy undoubtedly reminds us of the idea of the Platonic solids and especially the idea of the "hypercube" which states that a painting is the shadow of a three-dimensional cube, in the same way, that a cube is the shadow of a four-dimensional hypercube, each dimension would be the shadow of the higher dimension. Similarly, Plato affirmed that "material things are the shadows of ideas"; starting from this premise and taking into account that the "form" and the so-called "substance" are only projections, the only way to know the "truth", the ultimate (and first) reality would be knowing, experiencing and living the light that is the cause of the projection of the forms. It is there that the Neoplatonic mystic Plotinus expounded his "theory of hypostases". Hypostasis is the true substance, the true being, declares the theory of Plotinus, and whose structure is as follows: first hypostasis: "The Absolute One", second hypostasis: "Nous" (equivalent to Logos), third hypostasis: "Soul".

So, continuing with the text, to know the truth we simply need to live.

Coming now to the end of the book is where I want us to get more deeply into this thing of knowing the one truth. There is something inside me that wants to give you the answer, to give you the one truth, but there is also that other part that tells me that I have already done it, that, in creating this book, that "one truth" will manifest itself in the reader who can connect with it. And I will trust that.

Whether it is the patents and all the theories surrounding the Illuminati elite, the predictions of TV channels or a card game, the unidentified flying objects coming out of the ocean, on the moon, the sun, or in ancient paintings, EVERYTHING is a truth for the one who experiences it. The same goes for the placebo or nocebo effect or energy control powers such as levitation and many others not mentioned in this book. I repeat, everything is a manifestation of our projection. Shadows of reality.

THEY DO NOT WANT US TO WAKE UP

Given everything we have seen, it is even logical that the purpose of this elite that controls everything is that we do not wake up, that we do not know the truth, and that we do not think on our own. They know very well that we are very impressionable and they use this to their advantage. Apart from everything we have talked about, if this book can be of any use to you, it is for you to look inward, not so much outward. Maybe here we saw many things from the outside world, but that is not the main focus of the message that contains "the only truth". To stop being unconsciously controlled by everything that happens externally we must start by having control over our life. Such control comes with the responsibility that we can decide how we take things. This book is not material to empower you with anger because you are being controlled or because you are not being told everything that happens out there but to focus on the most important thing: yourself.

In this last chapter, we will talk about those people who were about to change things and ended up disappearing mysteriously. They were people who had many ideas and were carrying them out for the good of humanity, but from one moment to the next, they were never heard from again.

Let's dive into these stories, but again, it's not to think "how unfair, nothing can be done" but to remember that even if they want to control everything, the truth will always come out. You and I and the millions of others who will read this book are part of that change. We may not be able to do anything individually other than change our inner world, but if millions of people also change their inner selves and access the truth, then millions of beings transforming their inner selves are now indirectly transforming the outer world.

Three people who were to open our eyes, but mysteriously disappeared

Frank Suarez

The first one we will talk about is Dr. Frank Suarez, who died on February 25, 2021 after falling from the balcony of his ninth floor apartment in the Parque de Loyola condominium in Hato Rey, according to the Puerto Rico Police. The curious thing about his death is that it was just before launching his new book that would deal with the cure for cancer and metabolism.

Frank started to give negative comments towards pharmaceuticals, he did not recommend using such products as many ofthem could cause illnesses again since they usually contain many side effects. In other words, even if they work in the short term, in the long term they are not at all beneficial to thehuman body.

There are two versions of Frank's death. The first is the one that everyone knows since it was in the news, that he committed suicide by falling from the ninth floor from where he was staying. The authorities simply said that Frank took his own life because a year ago he was "taking depressants" because he simply felt very bad.

His friends and family did not agree with this because he had a lot of projects and things he
wanted to do. And this is where the second hypothesis appears.

Frank days before began to tell about the pharmacies and the medicines that people normally consumed explaining about the side effects and the profits that these pharmacies had in order to keep making more and more money. In a video he said the following: "With the information that we give here in Metabolism TV, with the idea that all of you are not victims of the System, victims of ignorance, the only defect of the body is that sometimes it has an ignorant owner". Frank went to a whiteboard and started explaining some things about the "10 most harmful drugs, the list of the most sold drugs and there really is no drug that is not harmful, there is no drug that does not have side effects". In a video titled "Episode #1200, Does it help me or harm me?", Frank explained that a famous doctor named 'Nicolas Gonzales' passed away suspiciously as he was working on naturally curative ways to cure cancer. Frank started mentioning that people were in danger when they tried to get into that section and that they died in mysterious ways, woke up lifeless and even fell from places where no one falls. This is where it all seems to come together.

Stanley Meyer

This is the case of one of the inventors who would have brought about a major change in the automotive industry.

Meyers was an American scientist who developed, manufactured and patented the first real alternative energy source to oil, using only tap water. Specifically, an engine capable of running a vehicle with only H2O as a source of energy.

His theory consisted of breaking the water molecule with positive kilowatt pulses at frequencies between 10 and 15 kilohertz. The mixture was then injected into the engine, which produced water again. It was not even necessary to recharge the engine with more liquid, since the component coming out of the exhaust pipe was recycled back into water autonomously, and only 7.4 microliters of water were needed for each explosion to generate 50 horsepower.

Stanley Meyers went on to work for NASA and was named inventor of the year in 1993. However, he died of poisoning under mysterious circumstances at the age of 57, one day before signing a multi-million-dollar contract with the U.S. Department of Defense. Some conspiracy theorists pointed to the oil industry as his killers, and even his brother claimed that months later Meyers' buggy and experimental equipment were stolen.

Jacob Grinberg

We talked about Jacob's discoveries in the previous chapter, but perhaps what the reader did not realize is that he was on this list of people who mysteriously disappeared. Jacob was directly concerned with many things that are still hidden from the general public. He was already testing the telepathy and psychic powers of human beings. This, although for you the reader is nothing new, Jacob's case is that he was spreading it all over the world and becoming very well known.

The scientist has been missing for more than 28 years, since December 8, 1994. The news was given by his family on December 12 of that year, as they had prepared a birthday celebration for him, but he never showed up. Although nothing is known about it, theories are that he could have been the victim of a crime, that his investigations disturbed the CIA and the FBI and even that he could have been abducted by extraterrestrials.

The end with all this is clear: there is a certain limit to our outer freedom, but there will never be a limit to our inner freedom. Death is nothing to fear. If anything, we should move away not from our purpose in life, but from wanting to fit into the mold prescribed by the elite.

There may not yet be a car that runs on water, there may not yet be the definitive book on the cure for cancer, there may not yet be telepathy
and other mental powers accessible to everyone, but these are just excuses. In reality, there are people with "supernatural" powers, there is a lot of information on how to prevent diseases and what they really are, and there are also many inventions that are revolutionizing human life. If you want to know about them, just put that on YouTube: "inventions that will revolutionize human life" or something like that. Of course, this book does not contain the whole truth, but it contains the only truth: that you create your own.

Man who cured 16 cancer patients with frequency and vibration

What is the nature of reality? The answer to this question is usually highly ignored by most of the population, but not for many scientists who managed to understand and demonstrate that everything is composed of energy, and by manipulating these subtle energetic forces we were able to transform ourselves and everything around us. Behind this, there was a man who wanted to use these forces of nature to cure all diseases and increase the overall health and longevity of mankind to a whole new level. This man's name is Royal Rife, a scientist who not only built the best microscope ever created capable of seeing a living virus and bacteria, but he cured 16 cancer patients he treated in just a couple of months using the power of frequency and vibration.

What this man generated at the time led to a group of 44 scientists meeting in 1931 to celebrate a revolutionary event they called "the end of disease," indicating that through Dr. Rife's discovery, it would be possible to treat any type of disease with a simple frequency- based device.

Royal discovered that every virus and bacterium had a particular frequency to which they were vulnerable, which he called the "lethal oscillatory rate," a term that is used today. After his discoveries, Rife tested the elimination of specific bacteria, viruses and tumors in rats by using this electromagnetic frequency, which ended up being a great success, so he ended up testing it on humans and was also successful.

This is what Royal Rife stated after its success:

"With frequency instrument treatment, no tissue is destroyed, no pain is felt, no noise is heard and no sensation is felt. A tube is turned on and 3 minutes later the treatment is complete. The virus or bacteria is destroyed, and the body recovers naturally from the toxic effect of the virus or bacteria. Several diseases can be treated simultaneously.

But if this happened almost 100 years ago, why are we still spending more than $185 billion on cancer treatments per year? Why do 1 in 3 men and 1 in 2 women suffer from this disease?

Well, not everything was going to end up being a fairy tale for such an invention that would have completely revolutionized human history. Years later, after Rife created his company in 1937, the head of the American Medical Association, a man named Morris Fishbain, immediately sent his lawyers to try to buy the exclusive rights to the technology that Rife and his engineers were working on. Rife, however, turned down the offer.

But apparently Mr. Morris was a man who had already accomplished such feats as you are to other inventors who endangered the monopoly of the pharmaceutical industry and large families like the Rockefellers, and he did not give up.

In the end, what Fishbain allegedly did was to fund one of the engineers working with Rife to create a lawsuit against him.

This was the beginning of the end for Rife and his machines as he collapsed and ended up in alcoholism. Then, no matter how much he won the case, the legal costs bankrupted him and his company went bankrupt.

Sometime later, Rife's lab was trashed and the police confiscated the rest of his research. It was basically as if this pioneering invention to cure cancer had never happened. And as we well know, today cancer is treated with ultra-expensive chemotherapy treatment that damages the human body far more than it cures it. The reality is that cancer treatments have killed far more people than they have cured, but we continue to believe that the purpose of this industry is to save us. You know I don't need to tell you the only truth because the only truth always ends up coming out since it was always right under our noses. Are you going to continue to believe that the people in control want healthy, growing people? If that were the case, why are they fluoridating all the water supplies? Why are they spraying the whole sky with chemicals? Why are they giving us genetically modified foods that contribute to disease? Even animals created for food are all the time being pumped full of all kinds of hormones and chemicals. How long are we going to keep blindfolds on believing that what we are being told is true? The truth is that there is something behind all this working from the shadows that do not want these developments to take place, but it is up to us to put an end to all this.

As George Orwell said:

"The masses never reveal themselves of their own free will, and they never reveal themselves simply because they are oppressed. As long as they are not allowed to have standards of comparison, they will never realize that they are oppressed."

MK Ultra: CIA's secret experiment revealed

The MK-ULTRA program, or MKULTRA, was the code name for a secret CIA chemical interrogation and mind control program run by the Scientific Intelligence Service. This official U.S. government program began in 1953 headed by Allen Dulles and Deputy Director Richard Helms.

A total of 149 subprojects were underway at 80 universities, medical centers, and three prisons in the U.S. and Canada, involving 185 researchers, 15 foundations, and numerous pharmaceutical companies. One subproject of his explored the possibility of "activating the human organism through remote control."

Most important of all, the main objective of brainwashing people to be used as informants and spies, but without knowing what was going on, prevailed. This continued at least until the late 1960s, with what was intended:

o   Learning how to condition people to avoid information being extracted from them by known means

o   Develop methods of interrogation to exercise control

o   Develop memory improvement techniques

o   Establish ways to prevent enemy control of agency personnel.

How did they do this? The program used U.S. citizens as guinea pigs. Evidence indicates that Project MK-ULTRA involved the illicit use of many types of medications, including drugs and other chemicals, sensory deprivation, as well as other methods, to manipulate individual mental states and alter brain function.

One of the drugs used in this "experiment" was 3-quinuclidinyl benzilate or BZ for short. This substance generates Alterations in the level of consciousness, misperceptions and difficulty interpreting (delusions, hallucinations) poor judgment and discernment, short attention span, absence of mentality, memory impairment (particularly short-term), and disorientation.

LSD was also used for a time, but because it provoked unpredictable reactions, it was abandoned.

Other substances used were temazepam (used under the code name MKSEARCH), heroin, morphine, MDMA, mescaline, psilocybin, scopolamine, marijuana, alcohol, sodium, and pentothal (also called truth serum).

Then MK-Ultra hypnosis was studied, and the aim of these experiments was the creation of "hypnotically induced anxiety" among many others. Several were involuntary guinea pigs, and those who accepted were poorly informed of the dangers.

Among some of the people who bear witness to these experiments is James Stanley, who was a career soldier when he was administered LSD in 1958 along with 1,000 other militaries "volunteers".

All suffered hallucinations, memory loss, incoherence, and severe personality changes. Stanley exhibited uncontrollable violence. It destroyed his family and inhibited his ability to work and he never knew why until the Army asked him to participate in a review study.

He sued for damages under the Federal Claims Act (FTCA), and his case went to the Supreme Court in United States v. Stanley. Debated and decided in 1987, the Court declared his claim unfounded (5-4), ruling that his injuries occurred during his military service. Justices Thurgood Marshall, William Brennan, and Sandra Day O'Conner wrote dissenting opinions, stating that the Nuremberg Code applies to soldiers as well as civilians. In 1996, Stanley received $400,000 in compensation, but no apology from the government.

Perhaps the best-known victim of MK-ULTRA is Frank Olsen, a biochemist working for the Army's Special Forces Operations Division at Fort Detrick, Maryland. On November 18, 1953, he was administered LSD. He immediately became agitated and completely paranoid. Nine days later, he allegedly committed suicide by jumping 13 stories to his death through a locked hotel window in New York City. His family members did not know he was drugged until MK-ULTRA was exposed in 1975.

The physical torture used in this program is based on the KUBARK Manuals, which is the official name of the so-called "Torture Manuals" used by the CIA and U.S. military forces, to this day. The following is a partial list of forms of torture:

- Confinement in boxes, cages, coffins, etc., or burial (often with oxygen venting or air tube)
- Hanging in painful positions or upside down
- Forced participation in human slavery

- Sleep deprivation
- Perceptual isolation (causes the victim not to feel the senses of sight, hearing, touch, taste, and smell).

- Pulled or displaced upper and lower extremities
- Near-death experiences, commonly asphyxia due to choking or drowning, with immediate resuscitation
- Surgery to torture, experiment, or provoke the perception of bombs or physical or spiritual implants.
- Application of snakes, arachnids, larvae, rodents (e.g., rats), and other animals to provoke feelings of fear, disgust, and repulsion;
- Victims are forced to perform or witness abuses, tortures, and sacrifices of people and animals, generally with sharp objects.
- In some cases, the victim is deliberately abused to become pregnant; the fetus is then aborted for any use, and sometimes the baby is taken for sacrifice or slavery.
- Leaving the victim hungry and thirsty for days, weeks, or months
- The victim is treated in a way that provokes an effect of spiritual mistreatment, which ends up making the victim feel possessed, persecuted, and internally controlled by "evil spirits" or "demons".
- Threats of harm to family, friends, loved ones, animals, and other victims to force compliance
- Use of illusion and virtual reality to confuse and create non-credible disclosures

Cleverly, Richard Helms, CIA director and chief architect of the program, ordered the destruction of all MK-ULTRA files before resigning in 1973.

Despite these precautions, some of these documents were not destroyed and were made public in the late 1970s. The documents highlighted the espionage agency's great cynicism. Faced with a possible investigation, the agency was quick to dismiss the significance of MK-ULTRA's success, saying it had made no real progress.

Miles Copeland, a veteran CIA agent, expressed his doubts about this. Copeland told a reporter that "the congressional committee that investigated these matters only got a rough idea of what happened." Another source within the espionage community says that after 1973, the CIA's efforts increasingly shifted to the psych electronic field. They could get nothing more out of narco-hypnosis.

Neuropsychologist Jose Delgado was researching electronic brain stimulation. By implanting a small probe into the brain, Delgado discovered that he could exert enormous power over the individual. Using a device called a "brain stimulator," which worked with FM radio waves, he could electronically control a wide range of emotions, including anger, sexual arousal, and fatigue.

The Watergate scandal in 1972 would begin to draw public attention to greater government impropriety. A December 1974 New York Times article alleged that the CIA had conducted illegal domestic activities on innocent U.S. citizens.

This article prompted a congressional investigation into the allegations and a committee was appointed to lead the inquiry. Senator Frank Church was named chairman of the committee appointed to it.

Approximately 20,000 documents related to Project MKULTRA survived the deliberate destruction because they were financial documents and were stored elsewhere (and subsequently ignored, in order of disposal).

Being financial, the documents would reveal little more than the players involved and how much was spent. The actual findings during the investigation would come from interviews conducted by the Church Committee with people involved in the case who wanted to talk. In 1977, the U.S. Senate released a report on the findings of Project MKUltra. Senator Ted Kennedy revealed to the U.S. that the CIA had been testing its experiment on unconscious citizens, that the tests involved LSD, and that there were no known deaths from the activities.

The CIA would later admit that the evidence made little scientific sense, since, among other reasons, the agents monitoring MKUltra were not qualified scientific observers.

The CIA claims that such experiments have been abandoned, but Victor Marchetti, a 14-year veteran CIA agent, has testified in several interviews that the CIA never stopped its research on human mind control, nor the use of drugs, but continually conducted sophisticated research. The very disinformation campaigns that are launched, through the media, false theories and conspiracy theories that can be ridiculed and discredited.

Victor Marchetti, in a 1977 interview, specifically expressed that the statements made that the CIA would have abandoned the illegal activities of MKULTRA after the inquiries, are themselves one more way of covering up the secret and clandestine projects that the CIA continues to operate, the MK-ULTRA revelations themselves and the subsequent statements of abandonment of the project would themselves be another device to divert attention from other clandestine activities and operations not disclosed by the Committees.

A follow-up report by the U.S. General Accounting Office in 1984 would reveal that, between 1940 and 1974, the CIA exposed thousands of human test subjects to dangerous substances. Of course, with no remaining program documents and few witnesses willing to talk, we will never know the exact number of victims.

What has grown up around MKultra is the theory that it is still being used today and is being used mainly on celebrities and people in high places, and that the program is run by the Illuminati.

This theory is based on videos where certain celebrities are seen having some kind of "glitches" or strange behaviors, which are associated with MKultra glitches. There are many videos about this kind of behavior that you can find on the internet that we suggest you look for if you want to check for yourself this theory. The question we can ask ourselves at this point is, in addition to using MKultra on celebrities, are they applying it on a worldwide scale on each of us without us realizing it?

The answer could be a big yes since once we understand how the brain works we realize that it is very programmable and manipulable, but here the point is to become conscious since a conscious mind is not possible to manipulate since it acquires its mental control.

FINAL REFLECTION

I chose the title to know the only truth to attract attention and produce a sudden shock in your mind. I do not have the only truth nor do I intend to have it at some point. As I was writing this book I wrote down in my notebook that I wanted others to read it because it conveyed a sense of joy in knowing the vastness and madness of the world we live in. Madness in a good sense, that sense that unsettles you and makes you rethink many things. This world is fantastic and I hope that now that you have finished reading the book you can consider it so. In this game of life I think the interesting thing is not to try to pass the game, or to win, or to fear losing, but simply to play. You are a character, but you are also the director of the movie you are creating. We all are, we all play, and we just take it so seriously that we forget to have fun. They say the truth will set you free, but first, it will bother you a little. I am aware that there are chapters and things that I have written here that can generate controversy and lead you to a point that you had not considered, or to complain, it doesn't matter, just remember something: your freedom does not depend on where you are, or with whom, but on how you think. You are the creator not of what happens to you, but of how you react to it. In a causal world, remember to take care of the cause and love the affections, whatever they are. I send you a big hug, may love be with you always, and may peace be in your days. Thank you for reading me.

BONUS

To access the gift books, just copy and pastethe following link in your browser and download the files

https://drive.google.com/drive/folders/1yhvQy wR2WTFjzwd_n8IDGn4Lls2qf8T4

DISRUPTIVE CONSCIOUSNESS

We are a company dedicated to the entertainment and dissemination of disruptive material to achieve in this way continue to expand human consciousness while enjoying this journey through the material world.

Life is a game, and we are here to play it. In the meantime, we continue to expand our minds to levels we could never have conceived of reaching before.

Our main objective is to reveal to the world all the information that lies hidden and forgotten in the deepest recesses of our planet. We all deserve to awaken the reality within us and experience a life of bliss and peace.

We are not against anyone, nor do we believe that a revolution is necessary where those who "have the power" are attacked, rather we believe in an understanding of love and unity as the foundation of our truth.

If you would like to be part of this movement, join the Telegram community Disruptive Consciousness where we share a lot of information free for our followers.

Scan the QR code with your cell phone and join the community.